Ghost Riders
of Upper Egypt

Ghost Riders
of Upper Egypt

A STUDY OF SPIRIT POSSESSION

Hans Alexander Winkler

Translated and introduced by
Nicholas S. Hopkins

The American University in Cairo Press
Cairo New York

Copyright © 2009 by
The American University in Cairo Press
113 Sharia Kasr el Aini, Cairo, Egypt
420 Fifth Avenue, New York, NY 10018
www.aucpress.com

First published in German in 1936 as *Die reitenden Geister der Toten*
Copyright © 1936 by Hans Alexander Winkler

Dar el Kutub No. 16761/08
ISBN 978 977 416 250 3

Dar el Kutub Cataloging-in-Publication Data

Winkler, H.A.
      Ghost Riders of Upper Egypt: A Study of Spirit Possession / Hans Alexander
Winkler; translated by Nicholas S. Hopkins.—Cairo: The American University in Cairo
Press, 2008
         p.   cm.
      ISBN 977 416 250 1
      1. Ghosts—Egypt   2. Ghosts—Saidis   I. Hopkins, Nicholas S. (trans.)
      II. Title
      398.250963

1 2 3 4 5 6 7 8   15 14 13 12 11 10 09

Designed by Andrea El-Akshar
Printed in Egypt

Contents

Introduction

Nicholas S. Hopkins

Ghost Riders of Upper Egypt is the translation of a book published in 1936 by the German anthropologist and specialist in comparative religion Hans Alexander Winkler. The expansive German title reads: *Die reitenden Geister der Toten: Eine Studie über die Besessenheit des 'Abd al-Radi und über Gespenster und Dämonen, Heilige und Verzückte, Totenkult und Priestertum in einem oberägyptischen Dorfe*; in other words, "Riding spirits of the dead: A study of the possession of 'Abd al-Radi and of ghosts and demons, saints and ecstatics, the cult of the dead and priesthood in an Upper Egyptian village." The imagery of the title refers to the notion that, in possession, the possessed is 'ridden' by the possessing spirit, the way a rider rides his mount. In this case the rider is the ghost of a deceased member of society, and the mount is a living person, metaphorically a camel. The central figure in the study, 'Abd al-Radi, plays the role of 'camel' to the ghost of his late uncle, Bakhit, who conveys messages—prophecies, diagnoses and cures, explanations of past events, and so on—to those who come to 'Abd al-Radi. We would now say that he 'channels' his late uncle. Or, in anthropological terminology, that he is a 'spirit medium.'

Scholars have identified several ways in which 'spirits' play a role in human society. Spirit mediumship is one such way, though not the only one. In spirit mediumship, the person possessed is considered an

1

intermediary between this world and another, while spirit possession implies that an external spirit has taken over a body and is controlling it, perhaps causing it to behave in unusual ways (Firth 1964: 247). Of course, the two can blend into each other. In the *zar* possession cult, as described here and elsewhere in Egypt, the spirits may afflict a person, requiring a form of curing in which an accommodation between spirit and human is reached, allowing the human to live a normal life outside the ceremonies. Typically in these cases, the spirit is invited into the body periodically to placate the spirit and renew the relationship. Both spirit possession and spirit mediumship often involve a form of trance in which the person's normal personality is replaced by another. Such a trance in turn can be distinguished from one in which the personality is simply absent, and a sense of nothingness, perhaps felt as an identity with God, prevails. The anthropological and psychological literature on spirit mediumship and spirit possession is of course much richer, and more analytically sophisticated, now than it was in Winkler's time, but Winkler's material is consistent with most modern interpretations.

'Abd al-Radi lived in the village of Naj' al-Hijayri, near the town of Qift, situated between Luxor and Qena in the governorate of Qena. Qift goes back to pharaonic times, as the ruins attest. It was one of the termini in the Nile Valley for the trade routes leading across the desert to the Red Sea. Naj' al-Hijayri was a relatively recent settlement near the edge of the desert to the east of Qift, and its inhabitants were distinguished from other villages nearby by being settled Bedouin rather than longtime farmers. In fact, there was little difference between these two groups other than a memory of a separate identity. Among other groups in the area were more recently settled Bedouin, the 'Azayza, and a community of 'Ababda. The origin of the 'Ababda is very contested, but they retain a sense of distinctiveness with respect to the Arabic-speaking groups; they are found in small groups throughout Upper Egypt. All these groups reflect the tendency of Bedouin to settle and become farmers, or to fill niches in agricultural society. All were joined together in certain social and cultural practices.

This multilayered study of the 1930s was precocious in its method and conclusions, and thus it retains its relevance today not only for Egyptian folklore but also for the history of anthropology in Egypt. In

Reem Saad

'Abd al-Radi's grandson displays a picture of his grandfather. Naj' al-Hijayri,
November 2006.

contrast to many other anthropological studies of that period, it is not just a list of details, but an effort to place a social process in cultural context—it is an extended case study. Winkler's careful ethnography highlights the time and the place of interviews and possession episodes. He recounts not only the history of 'Abd al-Radi but that of several other figures who came into view in the setting around him, some of them perhaps competitors for public attention. Winkler stresses the social process whereby an initial experience of possession evolves into a new example of a familiar social form—the spirit medium as the link between this world and the yonder one, and the social structure that grows up to enable this. The practices described here both reflect village social organization and lead to changes within it.

Winkler writes himself into the story, not only by recounting in the first person his interactions with 'Abd al-Radi and his entourage, but also by himself asking questions relating to his own family and life, so that he could evaluate the accuracy of the answers. Winkler details the growing personal relationship between himself and 'Abd al-Radi. Although there were enormous differences between the German scholar and the Egyptian farmer, there were also certain parallels—common age and family circumstance, and a life history that included low-paid labor (Hopkins 2007). The depiction of the relationship between the researcher and the informant is one of the more original themes of this book.

Winkler sometimes refers to his interlocutor as "'Abd al-Radi," at other times as "Bakhit," depending on his interpretation of the moment, as two distinct personalities successively occupy the same body. In fact, the spirit possession is more extensive, and the anthropologist shows how in fact multiple personalities appear in 'Abd al-Radi, although Bakhit remains the dominant one. He raises a possible interpretation in terms of 'Abd al-Radi's "split" personality, but does not develop the point. The analyses of the different mental crises people suffer certainly also raise questions for psychological anthropology, but Winkler deliberately stays away from psychology.

To describe the rise of this spirit medium, Winkler first establishes the cultural context through a review of all the options in belief open to peasants at this time. Thus he reviews how Upper Egyptians construct different forms of supernatural power, including the role of holy fools such as Bakhit presumably was in his lifetime. After all, ghosts, spirits, and suchlike are cultural categories, endowed with the ability to "act." This careful delineation of the cultural construction of the non-visible world provides the basis for his starting point of individuals and institutions. So Winkler analyzes not only the individual behavior of a snake-handler, but also the institutional framework—the role of the *zar* cult, and especially the place of the Sufi *tariqa*s and the *zikr*s they sponsor.

Winkler asks us to suspend our disbelief, and to focus instead on the interpersonal and institutional aspects of spirit mediumship. He places the messages of 'Abd al-Radi/Bakhit in the context of social dynamics, showing how the meaning is negotiated between the medium, the questioner, and others such as 'Abd al-Radi's father, Hamed, who often helped interpret the obscure statements of "Bakhit." The sessions with the "ghost" are thus occasions when meaning is developed and interpreted, as people seek new explanations within a shared cultural framework. Winkler devotes much space to the question of how far Bakhit's "messages" can be linked to the experience of 'Abd al-Radi, asking what this tells us about 'Abd al-Radi's consciousness; there are some challenging connections and gaps. What cannot be explained away by prior knowledge must also be dealt with by the analyst.

Winkler does not present the cultural dimension as seamless and monolithic, but identifies areas where there is disagreement, even skepticism, among people on the interpretation of the events to which they are witness. The approach to dealing with a person troubled psychologically was experimental, as friends, relatives, and neighbors argued about the correct interpretation and tried first one solution, then another. For instance, was 'Abd al-Radi really possessed by a ghost, or was it an *'afrit* or a *jinn*? What about 'Abbas, whose experience serves as a contrast to 'Abd al-Radi's? How is all this to be interpreted according to local understandings of correct Islam? People act in a local context of meaning, although they respond to different parts of the same pattern, and their negotiations in turn reinforce the meaning of different practices and institutions for other people. Winkler constantly stresses that all the interpretations and actions of people are predicated on the existence of God, whose power and will shape everything. Thus he argues that even extraordinary practices reinforce the centrality of Islam.

The sociopolitical context is largely missing from this study. We hear only hints about agriculture and labor migration, although both were important ingredients in village life, especially in a context in which the Depression was still felt. The European and colonial presence is essentially over the horizon, and so is any recognition of Egyptian politics of the 1930s. At the time of Winkler's research, Egypt was a protectorate with internal self-government. Perhaps because he was a German in English-dominated Egypt, or because he himself was an army veteran, Winkler often alludes to discussions of a looming war, but without further elaboration. In another book he reports at length a conversation in which his interlocutor argues that the Germans and the Turks should once again unite and force the English from Egypt, on the grounds that English rule abusively fostered the liberation of women (1936: 53). At the same time, however, we can note some of the patterns of tension in rural life, due to poverty, ill-health, and personal dilemmas of various sorts. Here it is noteworthy that the social role of 'Abd al-Radi/Bakhit was usually to advocate peace and reconciliation: he encouraged people to drop ideas of revenge and to settle quarrels over theft; he tried to get the bereaved to overcome their grief through positive actions; and he offered cures and solutions for their problems.

Winkler deliberately does not place this case study within the broader comparative framework, whether of Egyptology, psychology, or comparative religion. We follow his example, and leave that exercise to the reader. Winkler was interested in the comparative study of shamanism, of which spirit mediumship is a part. He had given a seminar on this topic in his last semester of teaching at the University of Tübingen. But here he retains the focus on the single case study, in a given time and place, stressing instead the social dynamics. The absence of material on other aspects of Naj' al-Hijayri life, except incidentally, makes it hard to include this study under the heading of functionalism, but it is at least a step in that direction.

The theme on which Winkler ends the book—the contrast between a European (Western) rationality and that of everyone else—also reflects what is certainly one of his underlying research questions: How does spirit mediumship work? Is it charlatanry, or is there a scientifically explainable core to this ability to see across time and space, or into the minds of others? What should we make of significant differences in religious experiences in various parts of the world? Winkler prefers to leave the question unanswered, merely saying that spirit mediumship cannot be entirely debunked, nor can it be proven. The question itself also reflects the influence of an older Tübingen colleague, the philosopher and psychologist T.K. Oesterreich (1889–1949), on him. Oesterreich's main interest was in telepathy and parapsychology, and to help develop his ideas he published a voluminous book of examples of possession and related phenomena in 1921, to which Winkler refers in his introduction. Winkler does not take the next step of phrasing the issue as one of a cultural construction of reality, in which things are true if people think they are. "Religious values . . . are true in their context" (Firth 1964: 239), and they influence action by framing the possible.

Winkler's ideas on the role of 'Abd al-Radi as a new "center" in village society were picked up by A.M. Hocart, an English anthropologist who was professor of sociology at Cairo University from 1934 to 1939. Hocart and Winkler overlapped in Cairo, and knew each other. Hocart was interested in the process of social evolution, and utilized Winkler's account to buttress his own analysis (1936: 300; see also Hopkins 2007: 416). We know that 'Abd al-Radi did not become the focus of a major shift in village social organization, but we also know that not too far away another religious ecstatic was able to create something much more enduring. In the village of Baghdadi, about 60 kilometers to the south, lived Ahmad Radwan, in whose name a major religious center emerged (Hoffman 1995: 255–67). The social insight was valid, even if the case of 'Abd al-Radi was a partial example.

One can also compare Winkler's book with the somewhat earlier account of Upper Egyptian mores, Winifred Blackman's *The Fellahin of Upper Egypt* (1927). Again, Winkler and Blackman overlapped in Cairo, and Winkler notes that he knew Blackman's book well, and expressed appreciation to her for encouraging him to persist in situating his research in Upper Egypt even when others counseled against it (1934: 2). Despite the many similar details in the two books, the approach is quite different— Blackman combed the area between Fayoum and Asyut and organized her material topically, while Winkler focused on a small area and produced an analysis that stresses the connections between the parts.

Hans Alexander Winkler was born in 1900, and served briefly in the German army at the end of the First World War. He then wanted to continue his studies, but, in the general postwar impoverishment, had to work as a laborer to support himself. He was drawn to communism, and for a while belonged to the German Communist Party. Then, as he developed an academic orientation he reduced his involvement in politics. He earned his PhD in 1925, and his habilitation in 1928, both in Tübingen. His field was comparative religion, and he also had a background in Orientalism, learning Arabic from the texts before he went to Egypt. However, his intellectual trajectory was in the direction of anthropology, and that might have developed further had it not been for the major interruption he suffered in 1933.

He was entering into a successful academic career when, in that year, the National Socialists (Nazis) took power, and purged him from the rolls of the university because of his prior communist affiliation. With the help of senior colleagues he was able to secure a modest amount of research funding and returned to Egypt in 1933 to continue the research he had begun the previous year. This was the moment when he met 'Abd al-Radi and analyzed his situation, during an intense three-month period from December 1933 to March 1934. Following that he traveled around Egypt, south to north and mostly on foot, for several months before returning to Germany. Later he returned to Egypt, and spent several years in the late 1930s working with an English expedition searching for and analyzing rock art in Egypt's deserts. During this time his wife died at the age of thirty-six, leaving two children. When war broke out in 1939 he returned to Germany and eventually entered the German diplomatic service (and necessarily joined the Nazi Party), acting for a while as liaison with the Arab politicians who had gathered in Berlin. In 1944 he volunteered for military service, and was killed in combat in Poland in January 1945. His survivors deposited many of his papers in the Tübingen University archives (see Junginger 1995a and 1995b).

Ghost Riders of Upper Egypt stands out in Winkler's work; it is unlike the books that preceded and succeeded it. It is in general much more congenial to contemporary anthropological tastes than his other two books based on ethnographic fieldwork in Egypt (Winkler 1934 and 1936). And of course it is different from the two works based on library research published before the fieldwork and the reports on rock art published in England in the late 1930s. It is not obvious why this book should have received so little recognition. Some may have objected to Winkler's sympathetic presentation of local beliefs, not grasping the methodological implications of placing oneself in the position of the Upper Egyptian peasants. The problem with the book is not language alone; even many German authors make little reference to it. The 1930s were of course a difficult time for German anthropology and comparative religion, and this book was both ahead of its time and also at cross-purposes with the dominant ideology. At the same time it was German, and non-Germans may not have realized how different this book was from that ideology, or they may have been preoccupied with other matters in those prewar years. Furthermore, Egypt was not yet firmly on

Nicholas S. Hopkins

The *tabut* of Shaykh Bakhit. His name is written on the cloth. Naj' al-Hijayri, November 2006.

the map of areas of interest for anthropology. One could probably count the number of anthropologists then specializing in Egyptian, or even Arab, matters on the fingers of both hands. For whatever reason, the book has always been an obscure reference, much more poorly known than it deserves to be—hence the importance of publishing an English translation in Egypt, after more than seventy years.

With the help of Dr. Reem Saad from the American University in Cairo, in 2006 I was able to pay a brief visit to the village of 'Abd al-Radi, Naj' al-Hijayri. We found there the grandsons of 'Abd al-Radi and their families. The shrine to Shaykh Bakhit had been recently refurbished, and now included also the *tabut* of Shaykh 'Abd al-Radi himself—both being buried elsewhere. We calculated that Shaykh 'Abd al-Radi must have died about 1970. We learned that the son of 'Abd al-Radi had in turn become a medium for Bakhit, but that since his death no one has taken up the role. Despite Winkler's comments on the sexual impotence that accompanies the role of medium, 'Abd al-Radi had married two more times since Winkler's study, and had numerous children. Likewise, his son had married and produced offspring. The sharp gender segregation Winkler described had clearly somewhat eased. Most of the employed in the family were local-level officials, not farmers, and appeared to be relatively prosperous, their equipment extending to cell phones and digital cameras. Thus the family social process started by 'Abd al-Radi (and his father Hamed) in 1933 was still continuing and evident seventy-three years later, although it had not had the social development into new institutions that Winkler had thought possible.

References

Blackman, Winifred S. 1927. *The Fellahin of Upper Egypt*. London: George G. Harrap; republished Cairo: The American University in Cairo, 2000.

Firth, Raymond. 1964. *Essays on Social Organization and Values*, London School of Economics, Monographs on Social Anthropology. London: The Athlone Press.

Hocart, A.M. 1936. *Kings and Councillors: An Essay in the Comparative Anatomy of Human Society*. Cairo: P. Barbey; republished Chicago, 1970.

Hoffman, Valerie. 1995. *Sufism, Mystics, and Saints in Modern Egypt*. Columbia: University of South Carolina Press.

Hopkins, Nicholas S. 2007. "Spirit Mediumship in Upper Egypt." *Anthropos* 102: 403–19.

Junginger, Horst. 1995a. "Ein Kapitel Religionswissenschaft während der NS-Zeit: Hans Alexander Winkler (1900–1945)." *Zeitschrift für Religionswissenschaft* 3: 137–61.

———. 1995b. "Das tragische Leben von Hans Alexander Winkler (1900–1945) und seiner armenischen Frau Hayastan (1901–1937)." *Bausteine zur Tübinger Universitätsgeschichte*, Folge 7, pp. 83–110.

Oesterreich, Traugott Konstantin. 1921. *Die Besessenheit*. Langensalza: Wendt und Klauvell. (English translation: *Possession, Demoniacal, and Other, among Primitive Races, in Antiquity, the Middle Ages and Modern Times* [London, 1930]).

Winkler, Hans Alexander. 1934. *Bauern zwischen Wasser und Wüste: Volkskundliches aus dem Dorfe Kiman in Oberägypten*. Stuttgart: W. Kohlhammer.

———. 1936. *Ägyptische Volkskunde*. Stuttgart: W. Kohlhammer.

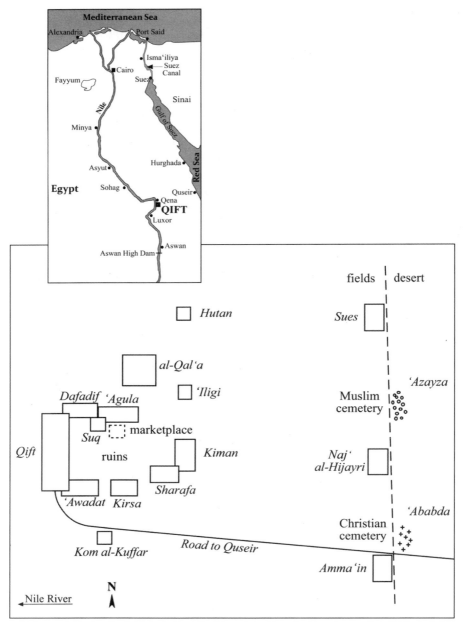

Sketch map of the area between Qift and the Eastern Desert (from Winkler 1934: 40), showing approximate locations of some settlements mentioned in the book.

Ghost Riders
of Upper Egypt

Preface

I remember vividly the impression made on me as a young student the first time I heard of the Siberian shamans. This was in a lecture by Alfred Bertholet in Göttingen. Since then I have always passionately studied the accounts of encounters and contacts of spiritually inclined persons with spirits, demons, and gods. In the summer semester of 1933 I myself taught on shamanism in the Department of the History of Religions in the University of Tübingen. Immediately afterward I traveled to Egypt.

I lived for a period in Cairo. Once I visited there, with a friend who was a painter, a man who could predict people's futures. Evening had already fallen. We strode through the old city. The alleys grew narrower and more winding. At last we found the house of the spirit medium. A gas lantern illuminated the stairs, so that one could make out the steps. Upstairs we found a very large room in which half a hundred men were sitting. They were talking softly together while waiting for the "shaykha," a man who had received his knowledge in fact from a she-demon. This is why people now called him the "shaykha." The room was brightly lit. Chairs were arranged along the walls. The floor was covered with mats. Two great old grandfather clocks were set opposite to one another. Their deep ticking sounded among the whispering of the people. A large model ship hung from the ceiling, and a brightly colored oil painting hung on the rear wall. In front of the waiting crowd a free space had been left for the spirit medium. Nearby sat a man with a pair of sugar loaves, which he was offering to the "shaykha" in thanks. Suddenly there was a movement in the crowd. The medium came out of a side door with a quick step, wearing a white robe, bareheaded with long dark-blond hair that fell in a disheveled way across his pale forehead. He had blue eyes. People had told me he was from the Maghreb. The most unusual feature was a silver hoop he had slung over his shoulder and chest like a French horn. Smiling and making faces, he sat down. A boy brought his water pipe. He took a couple of deep drafts, then winked at the guests in a satisfied way. In the background a pair of women were squatting; they seemed to be looking after him, and somehow to belong to him. Anyone who wanted something from the "shaykha" had to wrap up two piasters (no more and no less) in a handkerchief, which he would then hand over to the spirit medium. They also had to declare their names and their mothers' names, as well as the religious denomination. The spirit medium removed the money from the handkerchief and began to twist and squeeze the cloth, and also to sniff it. Then he began to whisper and occasionally stared at the floor, as though he saw someone there to whom he was speaking—who else would that be but the she-demon from beneath the earth? To the painter he said, "You are on a hunt, but your prey has evaded you. If you go on a trip, you will find your prey." To me he said, "You are looking for a treasure but you won't find one." To a third he predicted special luck in the coming days. To a fourth he denied an answer on this day. Perhaps the message is clearer and more meaningful to those who generally ask for advice than in the messages given to us Europeans. Of course it is possible to read anything into such oracular pronouncements. The "prey" could be a scientific goal, a winning lottery ticket, the completion of a deal, a girl, or some other kind of triumph. And who does not have some kind of hope in their heart that can be read into this oracle? And the same goes for a "treasure." Perhaps the man took me for an archaeologist or a savage grave robber or some other kind of treasure-seeker.

Later on when I came across 'Abd al-Radi, the subject of this book, I thought back to the "shaykha" in Cairo. In fact I had found a treasure. For it was a lucky chance that allowed me to meet 'Abd al-Radi. In general the intimate religious life of the fellahin is not known to the

European. He may live for weeks or even years in close contact with the fellahin, but he may not realize that in some nearby hut a spirit comes down into a human being, shakes and torments him, and then speaks through the mouth of this person about distant and hidden things. And even if the European learns something of this, and perhaps goes there and observes the possessed person, he is still very far from the spiritual life of the spirit-possessed and his guests. And so it was also by sheer luck that I was able over a period of many weeks to become so close to this 'Abd al-Radi that he accepted me as a friend, that he lost his timidity and let me look into his soul. And it was by still further chance that his family members also accepted me as a friend and took my work seriously, and even let me photograph 'Abd al-Radi while he was possessed. Thus I was able to gain an unusual insight into the religious life of Upper Egyptian peasants, a life that is actually quite different from how we imagined it to be among these Muslim peasants.

If a reader of this book should visit 'Abd al-Radi with the book in hand, I ask him one thing: do not show him the photographs of himself. I never allowed him to see his pictures while possessed. I did this out of a sense of tact, and I ask that this sense of tact be respected.

I have limited myself to presenting 'Abd al-Radi in his world. I could have sought out parallels from the ethnographic literature to adduce them. But that would have remained imperfect piecework. Whoever wishes to do this can find many cases in Oesterreich's book on possession, which I studied and learned from while in Upper Egypt. I have also decided not to seek parallels from ancient Egypt. And I have abstained from venturing into the domain of the psychologist and the medical doctor. I have concentrated on getting to know 'Abd al-Radi completely and on presenting him to the ethnologists, scholars of religion, Egyptologists, and psychologists.

In conclusion I respectfully thank the Emergency Research Fund for German Science, which made my work decisively easier both in the field and at the writing table, and the publisher, Dr. W. Kohlhammer, who found that the fruits of my labor were not too slight.

Hans Alexander Winkler
Cairo, December 28, 1935

PART ONE

The Environment
of 'Abd al-Radi

The Landscape and the People
around 'Abd al-Radi

Deep green fields on both sides of the railroad tracks, bordered on both east and west by the pale, yellow-gray mountains of the desert, overall a bright blue sky and a shining, burning sun—such is Upper Egypt. In the fields are scattered villages shaded by palms, brown clay houses growing out of the earth, here and there the whitewashed dome of a saint's shrine. The peasants in their long robes sit in the railroad cars, a bluish-white cloth artlessly folded on their head. Their faces are brown from the daily sun. In the east one can see a larger town, a thin minaret rising above palms and houses. This is Qift. The town used to be quite different, a big city with narrow streets and spacious temples, with merchants and peasants, priests and officials, soldiers and camel drivers from the desert. Their voices have fallen silent, their houses have collapsed. Only the name of the great Koptos is still linked to the speck of today—Qift.

Qift itself—a few pitiful dusty alleys, situated on the western edge of a huge field of ruins, covered with remains of worn walls, piles of stones, stumps of pillars, and numberless pottery shards. The whole place is grown over with prickly weeds, and where once the colorful life of a great trading center surged and swelled, today brown Bisharin and 'Ababda herders graze their wide-eyed camels. The field of ruins is lined by villages, and on the eastern edge lies Kiman, the 'heap,' in other

21

words, the heap of rubble. And on the eastern edge of this cluster stands the house of Muhammad Ahmad al-Sanusi. He was once one of the most skillful foremen working for German archaeologists. Now he spends the best part of the day sitting on a pile of rubble next to his black buffalo cow. I lived and worked in the house of this man in the spring of 1932 and in the winter of 1933–34. It was a comfortable place to live. The bustle and dust of the village did not penetrate this far, indeed the house bordered on the green fields, from which at night the heavy scent of the blooming beans or the odor of wet earth rose up. Sanusi resided with his wife and children in one half of the house, and his older brother, Shaykh Masri, with his family lived in the other. Masri used to keep a shop, but now only the big set of scales remained in front of empty shelves. To be sure, the gray-bearded shaykh often squatted behind the shop counter, but instead of tobacco or sugar cones, he now sold amulets to those who wanted to cure an illness of man or beast, to seek happiness in love, or to end torment by spirits.

The path to the nearby desert and the settlements along the desert fringe is not at all straight but is full of inexplicable twists and turns. The great dikes, which hold back the waters during the flood and simultaneously provide the links from one village to another, are intentionally built with many curves to withstand the water pressure, and all the small footpaths are equally sinuous. In the fields a buffalo-driven water-wheel creaks and sings, while a brown-skinned lad in a loose shirt runs behind the circling beast. Elsewhere, a fellah, muscular and naked to the waist, pulls the shaduf (a water-lifting device) up and down with persistent rhythm, and cries something like *"yahub ya juri minnak ya 'ud, yahub"* ("Oh, what tyranny you place on me, oh shaduf"). Many such melodies begin with the sigh that has become a word, *yahub*. Yet again a band of fellahin has spread out like guards over a plowed field; they break up the clods, which are as hard as rocks, with a short-handled hoe. Along the way stands a whitewashed *qubba*, a sanctuary; this one is a double shrine, dedicated to two saints. Over the door, on the wall, someone has drawn a red-brown man, holding a flag in his hand. Many such sanctuaries along the way, in villages and cemeteries, are decorated with such rough pictures, pictures of men, camels, trains, ships, birds, and other subjects that came into the mind of the artist. Over there, where the cultivated area ends and desert floor begins, stands a village, its entrance marked by date and doom palms. This is Naj' al-Hijayri. In this village lives 'Abd al-Radi, who was selected by the ghosts to carry them on his shoulders and to lend his voice to their messages.

Far from the hullabaloo of Europe, the peasant passes each day like the last, one year like the other. The hand of the peasant has created a fruitful Egypt. If this hand were stilled, the landscape would quickly change, the date palms would wither, the fields would turn into a hard desert floor where no crop would grow. But his hand does not rest, he plows and sows, chases away the birds, he threshes and winnows, and above all he irrigates, with his own power he lifts the shaduf to bring water from the bowels of the earth, or he drives his draft animal on the waterwheel, year in year out, often by day or by night. In this way, he created this landscape, but this landscape also created him, it supports him and his children. Rarely on earth do a land and a people agree to the same degree as Egypt and its fellahin. On either side of the narrow Nile Valley the peasant can see the pitiless desert. If he doesn't work, the desert will advance and bring death; if he does work, he can contain the desert in its boundaries, and with tenacious effort even gain new fields. He loves his land as he does his mother and his son, he values the heavy sweet water from the blessed Nile, and he fears the sinister, hostile desert.

In fact the people of Naj' al-Hijayri, who live on the desert edge, have not been settled here for long. Only a couple of centuries ago the ancestors of these peasants roamed as Arab Bedouin in the desert. But desert life is hard, and the mountains can only nourish a small human population. The green fields of the Nile Valley attract the eternally hungry herders. They come down from the mountains, marry fellahin women, and accommodate themselves to the law of the Egyptian earth according to which those who wish to settle must toil with the shaduf and drive the plow. These are two completely different worlds: the free life of hunger of the lonely herders in the endless desert, and the well-fed life of the fellah in the confining village. The descendants of the Bedouin in Naj' al-Hijayri farm just as skillfully as those whose ancestors were already here in the time of our forefather Adam. The Nile Valley is just as dear to them, and the desert as sinister, as to those whose ancestors were already cultivating the land in the days of the pharaohs. Bedouin can become fellahin in a short time, showing the constraining and assimilative power of the Nile Valley, which molds its people.

The field of vision of the fellahin is narrow. The axis in space is the Nile, and the axis in time is the Prophet Muhammad; they determine all happenings. That there might be countries whose people are not nurtured by the Nile does not enter their heads. And that there are reasonable people who do not strive for Muhammad's paradise seems incomprehensible. The daily thoughts of the fellah are directed to his work. A waterwheel must be repaired, a water buffalo is going to calve, a field must be harvested, fodder beans must be bought. The market is a weekly event. There the fellah takes his onions and radishes, sugar cane and grain, goats and calves, there he buys cloth and shoes, thread and spices, a holiday veil for his wife, a staff for himself. He may also have a tooth pulled, an amulet prepared, or a beautiful pattern tattooed on his hand. His life will be darkened by thoughts of the tax collector, who will appear at the place where the threshed and sieved grain lies in golden piles on the threshing floor. Thoughts of marriage make him happy, when the muffled hand drum sounds, the songs ring out, and the scent of boiled meat and festive bread fills his house. Or the birth of a son, announced through the womenfolk's trills of joy, brings joy to the father's heart—or yet again a circumcision feast, or a happy sacrifice at the shrine of a holy man, when the peasant redeems a vow. Death also interrupts the steady life of the fellah, when he hears from somewhere in a village the mourning cries of the quickly assembled women, and this signal is diffused throughout the countryside. Then he hastens to console friends and to help transport the corpse to the grave. Each one in the funeral procession must carry the bier for a few steps on his own shoulders. *"La illaha illa Allah wa Muhammadu rasulu Allah"* ("There is no god but God, and Muhammad is his prophet") chants the procession in an almost cheerful melody, to accompany a believing Muslim on the way to the compassionate Lord of the Worlds.

Politics and war, newspaper stories and stock market reports, discoveries and inventions—all these are far away, far from the vision of the Egyptian fellah. His eyes linger on the Nile and on the Prophet Muhammad.

'Abd al-Radi's
Religious Environment

Popular Religion and Islam

The thoughts of a people on the matters of the far side are everywhere various and of diverse origins, and not only among these fellahin. Many ideas from distant antiquity survive alongside recent ideas, some from abroad combine with old indigenous ideas. Only in the mind of a theologian can such abundance be organized: The scholar organizes the pattern of ideas around a figure, an ideal picture, incorporating many old ideas into the system with a new orientation, while much is simply omitted. The religious outlook of Upper Egyptian peasants appears quite different from that proposed by Muslim theology. It might seem that the fellahin have accepted Islam only very superficially, as though the old and local persist in uncontrolled freedom. This appearance misleads. The way in which Islam works only deepens the religiosity of the fellahin. Even though this depth does not often come out in daily life, it is there, and becomes visible in time of need. The clear prophecy of Muhammad brought no system, but a recognition and a goal: the image of the compassionate lord of the worlds. Many old religious thoughts and customs, fears, and superstitions remain alive among the people, indeed they are illuminated by the eternal God reigning in benevolent majesty until the end of the world.

25

The Human Body

The human body seems to us a sharply bounded and enclosed unity. With our microscope we penetrate into the smallest details of its structure, follow its transformations from the embryo in the mother's womb until its decomposition in the grave, we plunge deep into the spiritual, only to discover here also a physical basis, we calculate the manner and the performance capabilities of the physical and the spiritual, but in all this our research respects and claims the obvious—to us—borders of the individual. To the fellah, most of humanity past and present is on his side—the human appears not such a constricted individual, but rather physically and spiritually interwoven with powers from the other side. The boundaries can be traversed equally by influences from within and without.

The origin of the human is miraculous. Of the fecund sperm of man the first third falls to earth, the second third rises to heaven, and the third part enters the mother's womb and creates the human child. In the first month there, the sperm is water, in the second blood, and in the third flesh. After the third month the soul, *ruh*, enters the new child in his body through the fontanel. One can feel the soul through the throbbing of the newborn's fontanel. The third of the sperm that at the time of conception rises to heaven remains there until the settlement on the day of judgment—God and his messenger know how and why. The third that falls to earth passes—how, God and his messenger know—to the place where the man will die according to his fate. It is reunited with him in the grave. God only knows how. This is why people say, when someone dies far from home, "*tiltu*," "(This was) his third."

The fate of a person is written by God on the skull. Sutures in the skull represent this incomprehensible writing.

If a pregnant woman sees a stranger who impresses her through his beauty or ugliness or for any other reason, then the child in the womb can take on this beauty or other individual feature, especially because it is already moving in its mother's womb.

If a pregnant woman has a craving, for example for grapes or dates, and if this craving is not satisfied, then the image of the desired food can appear as a birthmark on the child's body.

When a woman gives birth to twins, whether of the same or opposite genders, the spirit of one and only one of them may turn into a cat. If possible, one should therefore give the twins in the first forty days after birth, in addition to mother's milk, some milk from a female camel to drink. In this way, this potential for transformation will be suspended. If there is no camel's milk available, then the spirit or soul of one of the two will wander about every night in the form of a cat. The body lies in place and sleeps. If the sleeping mother awakes and gropes around for the children's heads and through this movement wakes up the twin whose spirit has become a cat, then the child will die because its spirit, its soul, is at the time of waking absent from the body. The spirit that roams around in the form of a cat sniffs around in strange houses and nibbles on the food that it finds; the odor of the onion-spiced ghee sauce *(tagliya)* is especially appealing. Such a ghost-cat has no tail or a very short tail. It can happen that someone tries to kill this thieving ghost-cat in his house. If he really strikes it, he will not find a dead cat later. But the child, whose spirit the cat was, dies. The gender of the spirit-cat corresponds to that of the child—boys are tomcats and girls are female cats. After such a twin reaches maturity, its soul no longer wanders around in the form of a cat. However, such people retain the peculiarity that they are irresistibly attracted by food odors, especially that of *tagliya*—which is by far the most common kitchen odor in an Upper Egyptian village. If such a person smells *tagliya*, then they will immediately prepare it at home, or—if they do not have the means—they will request some from where they smelled it. If after such a stimulus they cannot get *tagliya*, they will fall sick.

People can sense many future events ahead of time, or know them through dreams, even though they cannot yet see or hear them.

If the right eyelid twitches, one will receive money, but if it is the left eye, then one will cry.

If the right palm of the hand itches, this is also a sign that money will come, but if the left one does, then one will have to spend money.

If something goes down the wrong way when a person is eating, then one of his kin is thinking of him.

If either of your ears is ringing, this is the *abul wuzzan*,[1] who weighs and measures the length of life. This is an *isharit al-mut*, a sign of death.

---

1 Either from *wzn*, to weigh, thus 'weigher,' or from *wdn*, ear, thus 'ear-man.'
HAW

One should put a finger in the ear and twist it around, to get the *abul wuzzan* to leave before he can weigh out the length of life. One should say, *huz huz—ruh la'guza wala 'aguz:* "*huz huz,*" probably a meaningless alliteration, "go to an old woman and an old man."

If one dreams that one has lost a molar tooth, then an adult will die, perhaps even the dreamer himself; if one loses an incisor in a dream, then a child will die.

If one sees someone in a dream as a dead person, this means that this person will enjoy particularly good health.

If one sees a living or a dead person in a dream in a lamentable state, or sick, tired, or naked, this is taken as a good sign. This means that this acquaintance, whether in this life or the next, is happy.

If one sees oneself naked in a dream, this means happiness and wealth.

If one sees a bride or a marriage, this means good luck.

If one dreams of a fire, this means that the place where the fire is in the dream will acquire luck and especially money. Fire comes from gold since both are red. It might even be worthwhile to dig for treasure in the spot indicated by the dream.

If the body can be influenced, it can also send out powerful signals.

A woman should not step over a strange child lying on the floor, for some of her monthly bleeding could fall on the child, and from then on it would have an incurable swelling, *gub*, on its head.

The bad smell of a man's sweat can enter the eye of another. This eye will then begin to burn. The afflicted one should then use his finger or a feather to bore into the ear, pick out a bit of earwax, and spread it on the eyelid of the inflamed eye like eye makeup. Then the *riha*, the evil 'influence' of the smell of sweat, disappears.

More serious is the evil eye, which many may cast, perhaps unwittingly. Especially the glance of admiration or envy of the envious one can be destructive. Children and cattle are protected against the eye by amulets, and houses by anything which attracts the glance, for instance a bird nailed over the door, perhaps a hoopoe, or a large lizard, or a colorful doll, or a crude sculpture of a man, or a drawing on the door, perhaps a man with a long hanging penis.

The mouth, the door of food, breath, and speech, is a hazardous entry point. This is why people should hold their hand in front of their mouth when they yawn, so that an evil spirit (*shaytan*) cannot enter.

Ghosts and Demons

If a man loses his life violently, then a spirit *('afrit)* comes 'out of the blood.'

In the archaeological site of Koptos and also in the nearby desert people excavate the saltpeter-rich soil that is then spread as fertilizer on their fields. Over time many have been killed in this task, buried in soil by collapsing pit walls.

The old Sanusi twice saw an *'afrit* in the same spot. He was then a young lad. Once he was passing through the ruins around midnight. He saw an *'afrit* standing on a high ruin. It resembled a white cloth, about knee-high. It grew steadily higher and higher, higher than the ruins, which equaled the height of two men. When an *'afrit* grows too tall, it bends completely over the man and squeezes him to death, at least if he is someone born under an unlucky star *(nigmu khafif)*. As the *'afrit* grows it makes the sound *totototo*. It was not possible to recognize a face or some other identifying mark; only something tall and white was visible and this sound was audible. So Sanusi uttered the *basmala*, "In the name of God, the merciful, the compassionate," and kept walking. Then the *'afrit* diminished and disappeared into the earth. At this point, Sanusi heard something like the clatter of many falling potsherds, *lulululu*.

One night a year later, Sanusi saw another *'afrit* in the same spot. It resembled a dog or a cat. In the dark it was hard to be more precise. Sanusi did not think anything of it, and took it for an animal familiar and said, *"ruh ya shaykh"* ("disappear, honored one"). Thereupon the ghost spoke with a deep voice, *"ruh ya shaykh."* Fear overcame Sanusi, and he quickly said the *basmala*. The spook then disappeared again. Sanusi noted that "the ancient Egyptians made pictures of the *'afarit*." He took out a small image of Bes sculpted in stone, and said, "Someone saw such an *'afrit* and then made this figure."

Half an hour from Naj' al-Hijayri in the desert there are a few ruins. A generation ago there were substantial houses in which European archaeologists worked. Near these ruins good saltpeter earth is found, so that the whole area is full of deep pits. Here twelve men were buried alive by the mountain. Many have already seen their ghosts. They have a donkey's arms and legs.

The father of 'Abd al-Radi saw such ghosts with a similarly monstrous aspect, many years ago when he was about thirty years old, and was collecting fertilizer in the Koptos ruins. It was nighttime, about 2 a.m. He had lain down for a bit. Then he suddenly caught sight of seven *'afrit* which had donkeys' feet and had eyes at the top of the skull. The *'afrit* sat down on his donkey. Just then his fellow worker came and the whole troupe of spooks disappeared.

A man from Naj' al-Hijayri went to Isma'iliya to work as a digger, as did many others from this area. One day this man was walking along the canal. There were many trees. Suddenly an *'afrit* jumped on his back, and the shameful one did with him what a man does with a woman. Thereupon the man could no longer speak; the next morning he could only babble. So a scholar was called, and he recited strong pious passages. The evil disappeared and the man's speech returned.

Another man from the village saw a *'afrit* as he was working with the waterwheel at night. Something was always preceding the circling camel. The man took a knife, held it bravely up to the spirit, and said, "Go away, you devil." The spook disappeared, since spirits fear iron.

The blood of a man who died a violent death can give rise to such spirits. Sometimes one can hear people say directly, "He who died a violent death becomes an *'afrit*."

These ghosts are thus closely tied to a person, as if they sprouted from a person—as if a part split off from the soul, when it suddenly and unexpectedly is forced to pass into the other world because of that person's violent death. But there are other spirits, independent of humans, that grow from their own roots, to people the world. The real residence of these spirits is under the earth. People call these *jinn* or *jinni* (pl. *jinun*, coll. *jinn*, which can also be used in the singular). As a people they are also called "those below" (*tahtaniyin*). They lie in wait for an opportunity to rob humans. Their only power is over the dishonest.

Two peasants had threshed sorghum (*dura*) on their threshing floor in the fields. It was nighttime. One of them went away. Then the other stole some of the undivided harvest that belonged to the two of them together. But through his dishonesty he gave those beneath the earth their power. The man lay down to sleep. "Those below" came out and stole some grain in turn. The first peasant then returned. He saw many little fellows with high-peaked caps (*tartur*, pl. *taratir*), who were doing something with the piles of grain. He said the *basmala* a couple of times, and they disappeared. He woke up his companion, and said to him, "Which of us was dishonest? I saw how the ones below were doing something with the harvest." The man denied having stolen anything. Thereupon, all the harvest vanished—those from below took it for themselves.

Overall, "those below" gain power from the dishonesty of a person. When someone steals, even when a woman in the house puts just a piece of bread on the side behind the back of another, then the ones from below come and steal ten times as much. After such an act, they return home.

A peasant was working with eight others. He was honest and pious. To till their field they used a shaduf and a well. Each of the peasants contributed to the purchase of the individual parts. As the crop in the field had been harvested and threshed, and the grain had been divided up, the account of the shaduf had to be settled, so the peasants sat down together beside it. The honest man raised his voice and pronounced the *Fatiha* (the first *sura* of the Qur'an, the "Lord's Prayer" of the Muslims). Then he calculated the expenditure and in the end he said, "Half a penny or a millieme is left over." As he said that, they heard a plaintive voice, "That will turn you into orphans, my children." This was the voice of those from below, who had hoped that the man would keep the millieme for himself. In this way he would have given those below the possibility of stealing some of the grain for themselves. The honest man answered the underground voice: "We ourselves are nine; you can be the tenth, so long as you leave the grain alone." The underground voice responded, "This is good." Thereupon the peasants began to measure the grain by bushels, and to divide it up. The honest man turned to the underground one and asked, "Where shall we put your share?" He answered, "Put it in the middle of the threshing floor and leave it there." So the nine men each took his part, and left a share in the middle. Then they went away. One of them turned around for a look, and saw how the underground one stood next to his pile, and then sank into the earth with it.

Among the demons one finds, as on earth, Muslims and Christians. In Qift lives a man to whom a Christian female demon (*jinniya*) had proposed marriage. However, as a Muslim the man rejected the marriage, but instead took her into his service. She took care of shopping for the man; for instance, she would bring a sugar loaf from the store. No one sees her; suddenly the sugar loaf disappears and the money for it lies in the cash box. Where there is a dishonest person, perhaps a helper in a shop or a servant in a house, she begins to steal from this shop or house. She then delivers the stolen goods to her friend, the man she serves. The demon also prophesies in this man's house. People come by to ask her questions. The clients are in one room, and the demon in another. People can hear her voice, and can also see her arm. If one gives her a gift she disappears under the earth among her own people.

Old Sanusi remembers the following from his childhood. In the village of Jiziriya near Abnud lives an old fellah, Haddad by name. He was called if anyone fell sick. This happened once when Sanusi was young. The old man asked for a basin filled with water, squatted down, and placed the basin in front of himself. Then he spread a large shawl, such as women wear, over himself and the bowl. Shortly he could be heard speaking with the underground folk, who appeared to him in or on the water. One could clearly distinguish his own voice and the small, thin voice of the underground folk. Sometimes the voices of the underground folk sounded disputatious. The conjuror then commanded them, "*balash al-kalam*": "That's enough talk. I want a cure for the illness of such and such a woman." The underground folk gave him their treatment for the illness, and the man prescribed accordingly. Incense was also used during the conjuration. However, Sanusi could not remember any more details, such as when and how.

Rais Khalifa had a noteworthy handgrip, heavy as lead. People knew that he had a mysterious strength. He could bend railroad rails, snap tamarisk beams, break coins as easily as bread, carry loads that otherwise would require six men. He says that as a child, he had always taken Hufni, a strong man, as role model, and he wanted to be as strong. People whispered that as a child he had stolen an entire camel load of grain for his mother. He was unable to lift this load. Then he heard a voice saying "*khud*"—"take"—and an unknown, strange power lifted the bag onto his shoulders. Since that time he has this peculiar strength at his disposition.

In the village of al-Qal'a lives a man who also had a spirit as a servant, a *khadim*. The demon supplies his master with money. People think that this money is good and accept it in payment. When they get home and fumble for the money in their pocket, they find only a few potsherds.

Other spirits do not think of serving people. Instead they approach them from the outset with the intention of hurting them. For example, there is the *qarina* (pl. *qarain*). If all the children of a married couple die one after the other, they begin to think that the *qarina* is responsible for this. So they may decide to sacrifice an animal as an offering to the demoness. Of course, a sacrifice to something evil is a sin. The animal must be completely black. It is slaughtered without uttering any of the sacred formulas that would ordinarily be used. The sacrificial animal is eaten without salt, and also the soup should have no salt. No one can speak during the meal. The bones are carefully gathered together, and they are buried in the house of the one afflicted by the *qarina*.

Other demons attack a man and half lame him. Such a man often dies before long. Or they twist the neck of a man, so that he must always hold his head stiffly in one direction. For such illnesses people look for *ambar/ambra* (ambergris) to effect a cure.

A few years ago a man in the neighboring town of Qus was possessed by a *jinn*. He had gone to a mosque toilet and had lit up a cigarette. At that moment there was suddenly a great clap of thunder. The man took fright, and in this instant a *jinn* entered him. These demons are omnipresent, and the moment when a man takes fright provides the best opportunity for a *jinn* to enter into him, usually through the mouth. How this *jinn* had entered into him, this man could no longer say, but he became sick and weak. Several scholars went to a lot of trouble, using the recitation of the Qur'an and other pious expressions to drive out the evil guest. All of this was in vain. Meanwhile, one day the demon explained through the mouth of the possessed that he was ready to leave him, provided Shaykh Hufni from Kiman was there. Some wanted to go immediately to fetch this scholar. But the demon said, "Remain here, Shaykh Hufni is in Qena right now (the provincial capital), but he will come today on his own." And in fact, Shaykh Hufni came after the time of the afternoon prayer in order to pay a sick call on the possessed man. The demon greeted him through the mouth of the man and said, "I was your fellow student. I studied with you in the al-Azhar Mosque in Cairo." The demon then exactly described a certain day, and the spot where Hufni stood then. "I was standing in such and such a place very near to you, probably you didn't see me because you sons of Adam can't see us." The demon then recited a passage from the Qur'an, said he would soon leave, and asked Hufni to remain with the man about two more hours, for there was a danger that right after his departure another *jinn* would enter the abandoned body. Then the demon exited, the man regained his former health, and no longer suffered from demons. The demon had remained in him for a couple of weeks.

A special class of demons threatens women in particular. These are the spirits of the *zar*, of foreign origin. An *'abd*, a descendant of a black slave, in Naj' al-Hijayri explained: "The *zar* comes from the Sudan, from the Barabra, in other words the Nubians. *Zar* spread in the country only after the coming of the Europeans, and it began to ride the daughters of the Arabs. These spirits were originally called *zarr*, and in Egypt that became *zar* for the first time. If a woman gazes at herself in the mirror too long and with self-admiration and primps herself, then the *zar* spirit uses this opportunity to penetrate her, he clothes himself with her." On the other hand, an old woman claimed, "Only if a woman has many cares or sorrows can the *zar* gain power, for example if a woman grieves too much for her dead husband or a dead child, or if she is threatened by unhappiness or cares." When a *zar* enters a woman, she falls sick, she suffers from eye aches, joint pains, deafness, or diarrhea—if not one thing then another—and in the economic life she is no longer good for much. The *zar* may also possess a man, but more rarely. In order to exorcise such a spirit, someone calls together all the *zar* members; they drum and sing and recite the names of the different *zar* spirits, such as Lulubiya, Magharba, Muj al-Bahr, Wullad, Umm al-Ghulam, Safina, Mama, or Maruma. Everything is arranged in a festive way for a *zar* exorcism. In addition to music there is also rich and tasty food; the guests and especially the *zar*-afflicted one are dressed and bejeweled as beautifully as possible. With the help of this feast and the songs the *zar* spirit is induced to reveal itself. Each spirit has its own tune: When the tune is played it answers through the mouth of the possessed and demands something for the afflicted victim, usually a pretty dress or a piece of jewelry. When the wish is granted, the pain of the afflicted one improves. However, the *zar* spirit remains in her or near her.

These *zar* spirits sometimes maintain a love relationship with the women. A man wondered why his wife adorned herself every Saturday and Sunday eve, while she went around the rest of the week in dull everyday clothes. He observed his wife for a while. Then one Saturday eve he went to her and wanted to spend the night with her. She asked him to leave her alone. The man asked why she didn't want him. So she said, "The *zar* visits me on these two nights." The man got angry and took his wife to the *qadi* (judge). He told the *qadi*, "I have a partner in marriage. In the future I am only going to pay the household expenses for my wife for half the month. The *zar* can look after her during the other half." The woman agreed to this.

When a woman is possessed by a *zar* or another spirit people say that the *zar* clothes itself in her; the *zar* is then in the woman like a man in his robe. Or people may say, the *zar* rides her; the *zar* sits on her like a rider on his mount.

People often see a whirlwind *(za'bula)* in the nearby desert or along the paths between the fields. A devil is the cause of this, and hides inside. No one knows how to protect against this.

Many people can manage with the spirits, either because they expel them or because they take them into their service. Such a power can come from one of two sources, either as a favor from God, and then people say: such a man has *sirr*, 'secret or secret favor.' Or the power can have a demonic origin, and then people say, this man has *ism*, 'name,' in other words he knows the names or the magic words of the demons. The man who, with the help of demonic strength, can break tamarisk beams, or the one who has a truth-telling she-demon at his disposal, or again the man to whom his spirit brings magical money that later turns into shards, all have *ism*. Holy, pious men have *sirr*.

Shaykh Masri, the brother of Sanusi, is one of those who know the names of the demons. When a poltergeist, whether called forth by an *'afrit* or a *jinn*, appears anywhere and throws tiles at people in their houses or tosses dung in people's faces, Shaykh Masri is called in. Masri then arrests the mischief-maker in the home. If he receives his honorarium, he expels the poltergeist immediately. But if he is not given his honorarium, he frees the spook after a week. Masri got his magical knowledge from books dealing with the magical strength of the names of God and from certain passages in the Qur'an that discuss the names and saying of demons. This is *ism*.

I was there once when Shaykh Masri was consulted. He was squatting on a mat in front of his door. On this door were seven hand prints in a row—the gesture of the hand with spread fingers to fend off evil. After a while a poor woman came and handed the cap of her sick son to the Shaykh as *riba*, a token. She had wrapped up a piaster in the cap as an honorarium. Masri moved closer to the woman, took the cap, and removed the coin. He said, "The youth has been in the north." The woman nodded. "Is he coughing?" "Yes." Masri examined the coin. "Why so little? This is a difficult illness. If you go to the doctor, you will end up paying much more." The woman said she would bring more money if he could restore health to the youth. Masri took a scrap of paper, a pen, and ink. "What is the youth's name?" "Sulayman." He added together the numerical value of the letters of his name. Then he calculated another number from this one. I was not able to learn how, but the fact that the consultation took place on a Friday played a part in this. Next to this number, he scrawled a couple of lines in Arabic script, skipped a space, and wrote the seven seals which symbolize the highest name of God, adding a couple of alphabetic compositions, then he skipped down further and wrote several further alphabetic compositions. Then he tore the paper scrap into three parts following the three separated parts. He gave the first one to her and said, "Throw black caraway seeds into cow ghee, then spread ghee over the child's body with this paper. Then take the second scrap, burn it together with the incense *mai'a (Styrax officinalis)* and cense the youth's body." Masri folded the third scrap together, wrote on each side of this packet a pentagram, and said, "The kid should carry this in his cap. Then bring him here, so that I can pursue this. This is a difficult illness, bring money."

Magic and Ordeals

Many older spells work independently, without the help of spirits.

If a raven or one of the kites that are always circling over the village steals a pigeon, then one catches such a thief and nails it visibly on the roof or a wall of the house to scare off future would-be robbers.

There is clearly a magical effect in the following: If something is stolen and one suspects a particular thief, then you buy a new waterskin, or *girba*, speak the name of the presumed thief together with the names of both his father and his mother, blow up the skin, and tie it shut. Then you go to the suspect. If he is the thief, you will see that his whole body is swollen. You say to him, "Return the stolen goods." Maybe he will answer, "I didn't steal anything." Then you go back and pump the skin up even more. You go back to the thief and say, "Give it back." If he gives it back, you release the air from the skin. The thief becomes healthy again. If he is still lying, you beat the skin with sticks. If he still lies you tell him, "You will die, hand it over." If all this is in vain, you stick a knife into the bag, and the man dies. If the suspicion turns out to be false, the spell will not work. Then you see that he is not guilty.

Another form of investigation into robbery is originally an ordeal. In the nearby village of al-Qal'a lives an old man, Hasan. You can turn to him when you want to identify a thief. Hasan then walks through the quarter where the robbery took place and where the thief is to be sought. He strides and sings special sayings (I was unable to find out anything about them), calls all those on whom suspicion might fall, and convokes them to him at a certain time the next day. Then he heats up a peasant hoe until it is red hot, and invites each of the suspects to lick it if he is not guilty. He assures them that the heat cannot harm the innocent. The one who refuses is the thief.

Magic spells and belief in spirits come together in the following ordeal. Old Sanusi told me about this. There is a book in which all the cures in the world are written down. This book is called 'Bukhari.' If several people are accused of an evil deed, they are asked one after the other to place their hand on this book, and swear, for instance in the case of theft, "I did not take it." If one swears a false oath on the Bukhari, this man will not live out the year: "Bukhari brings him in." He dies, and moreover, his wife and children also die one after the other; Bukhari exterminates the whole family.

Folk Medicine

Usually the fellah keeps a few drugs for curing at home. He buys them in the market or from a street peddler; there are few shops. Buyers and sellers wander from village to village, and their street calls are part of the music of the day, along with the voices of men and especially women and children, the barking of dogs, the cackling of hens, the rasping bellow of the water buffalo, and angry groans of the camels, the hideous braying of the donkey, and the nasal squeaking of the waterwheel. Sometimes an 'Ababda hawker passes by. In the sack on his donkey are his wares. He passes through the alleys and sings out in a sustained chant, "*al-kammun wa-l-samar wa-l-kusbara wa-l-shih—fi-l-bayt malih*" ("Caraway, fennel, coriander, and *shih*—lovely in the house").

The caraway, which he extols, comes in two sorts, white caraway as a kitchen spice, and black to protect from all kinds of sorcery. If a child is struck by the evil eye or touched by a devil, the black caraway will be crushed in a pestle, and the powder is mixed with clarified butter and rubbed into the body of the child. If a man is threatened by such devilish work, he will place some black caraway in his head covering, while a woman who is bothered by spirits will entwine it into the plaits of her hair.

Shamar, fennel, is used for a cough, but also for stomachaches and limb pains. You prepare a decoction and drink it.

Kusbara, coriander, is used for incense. If someone is sick, he searches for coriander and burns a dry cow patty, the usual combustible material in the house. When it heats up, he sprinkles coriander on it, and crouches over it.

Shih, the fruit of a variety of Artemesia, is spread by the peasant in front of the house to drive out vermin.

Lamun, lime, is also known as a healing substance, useful for all diseases. It also 'cools the blood,' so men avoid it when they are going to their wives.

Another street peddler carries a whole medicine chest, and calls out to the women, "*Al-faih ya banot al-kohli ya banot is-sabun ya banot al-filfil ya banot al-gunzara ya banot falali ya banot mustika ja banot mihlab ya banot grunful ya banot.*"

Ya benot, in other words, *ya banat*, "you daughters (you girls, you women)." The street caller stretches and stresses heavily the second syllable, and this produces the 'o' in *banot*. Many street calls are elongated in this way, and often an 'a' turns into an 'o.'

The splendors that the itinerant pharmacist advertises are partly curative.

Faih is a powdery perfume. Women stir it in clarified butter and smear it on themselves. Men sprinkle it in dry form on their clothes.

Kohl, the famous powder of antimony, is the best thing for the eyes. You apply it to the edge of the eyelids. This is also used as a cosmetic.

Sabun is soap, *filfil* pepper.

Gunzara, verdigris, is for the eyes. Especially if a child has pus in its eyes, the eyes are anointed with it; if the pus is in the ears, some drops are put in the ear—"it kills the worms," and such inflammations are thought to be caused by worms. Sometimes a woman comes to market and rubs the eyes of the children with the palm of her hand, and the worms fall out. Unfortunately I never had a chance to see this woman.

Fallaya (pl. *falali*), are small wooden dust combs which are mostly used to remove lice from the hair.

Mastika, mastic, is also used for incense, with which you can 'smoke out' a stinky, musty room.

Mihlab (*Prunus mahaleb*, St. Lucie Cherry) are said to be the fruits of a foreign tree from which you can also cut the strong peasant staffs known as *shuma* (pl. *shuwam*). The seeds are crushed in the pestle and added to the holiday baking. Women also use it in powdered form, in clarified butter, as ointment for the body. They also like to chew *mihlab* seeds. Sometimes they anoint the face and body with the spittle-juice as a kind of perfume. My informant, old Sanusi, tried to explain this, his hands in his armpits.

Grunful (clove) is a spice valued as perfume.

Another cure you can fetch from a specialist: If you get a splinter under your skin, you should swab the area with a daub of cotton and snake fat. In this way the splinter will come out of its own accord in two or three days. A man in the neighborhood known as Dafadif has this snake fat in stock. He butchers dead snakes and removes the fat, which he sells for a high price.

If a donkey has a wound from his loads, you should burn the sole of an old shoe and spread the ashes on the wound. The donkey will then recover in a week.

The fellah is helpless in dealing with snakebites and scorpion stings, but there are people who can help. One of them is Hajj Ibrahim. He cannot read or write. Snakes and scorpions obey him. If there is a snake anywhere in a house or in a straw mattress, for example, or even the suspicion that one is there, then people call for Ibrahim. He comes, whistles, and turns his head in all directions, then he says, "Come." The snake then comes to him, and he takes it away. He does not whistle for a scorpion; instead he gestures with his finger and calls him, "Come." And the scorpion crawls out. Ibrahim does not harm the animals—he feeds eggs to the snakes when he can. When he has a sackful of such creatures, he travels with it to Cairo and delivers it to the zoo. Others say that he frees them in the desert. One time he took the train to Cairo, with his sack. The conductor came. Ibrahim did not have a ticket. The conductor told him to get off the train. So Ibrahim opened up his sack of poisons, and the snakes and scorpions crawled out. Thereupon the conductor and the other travelers asked him to close them up in the sack again. In this way he completed the trip without a ticket.

His mother was annoyed because he was always bringing these poisonous creatures home. One time he brought a rather large scorpion, and she scolded him. So Ibrahim told his mother, "Today he is going to sting you." Then he went out, but soon people came after him and said, "The scorpion stung your mother." The mother screamed and cried from pain. He stroked the wound with his hand, and the pain disappeared. Since then the mother has not said anything. Some people say that Hajj Ibrahim has his skill as a blessing from God; others say he knows the names of the demons who help him. Ibrahim is also consulted when a cow has swallowed a thorn or something similar, and this has gotten stuck in her throat. By stroking, he can extract the thorn.

The Shaykh Cult: The Holy and the Dead

The shaykh cult occupies a central position in Upper Egyptian folk religion. Let us examine the uses of the word *shaykh* (pl. *mashayikh*), in our research area. The closest translation would be 'honored' or 'venerated.'

1. Shaykh is first of all the honorable form of address for an adult Bedouin, or even a settled Bedouin, or even someone who has been a fellah for a long time but who claims Bedouin origins.

2. Shaykh is the title of the headman in the smallest village community, a village quarter, ranked under the mayor, *'umda*. Similarly, the chief of the settled Bedouins on the desert edge would carry the same title, with the same meaning.

3. Shaykh can be used ironically as an angry form of address to anyone. For instance, a father can say to his son, "*ruh ya shaykh*," meaning, "Get out of here, my dear." In the example given above of the meeting with the ghost-dog, Sanusi used the same expression to the apparent dog.

4. Shaykh is the title of a man who knows the Qur'an and the Traditions, one might even say, anyone who can read and write. This knowledge might actually be quite modest.

5. Shaykh refers to pious people who have rendered services to Islam, often outstanding men with special powers of bygone times. Especially striking among these are those who founded a Sufi order or the branch of an order, *tariqa*.

6. Shaykh can mean fools, whose folly somehow has its origin in God, be it that the origin is in dispassionate gentleness, in the mysterious anticipation of coming events, in successful appeals in prayer, or somehow merely indicates that those who show disrespect for the fool encounter some kind of accident.

7. People are called shaykh when they distinguish themselves by a special power, for instance, snake charmers or magicians.

8. It is not uncommon that a man or a woman is seized by the ghost of a dead person, and becomes possessed. The ghost then speaks through the mouth of the one possessed. If a ghost announces its presence in this way, he is henceforth called shaykh.

9. Shaykh is also used to refer to the man (*shaykha* for a woman) in whom such a ghost appears, 'on whom he descends.'

10. Shaykh finally refers to the tomb or the sanctuary established for a holy person, a scholar, or a miracle-working ghost.

Consequently, we can distinguish between religious and profane shaykhs. Here we focus on the religious ones.

Shaykhs—from the great theologians and mystics of the past right on down to the holy village fools—appear as border-people between this narrow world of everyday fatigue, sorrow, and need and the invisible world of God and the spirits.

The fellah honors the holy fools, the itinerant bringer of blessings. He offers hospitality and lets him sleep in his house, and hopes in this way that God will be pleased; he hopes that blessings will be directed to him. The fellah trembles when a ghost appears in a possessed person, and he tries to appease him and to be friendly, for instance, mostly by building a worthy grave monument or a sanctuary for the one who is revealed. And these grave monuments and sanctuaries then become central points of the religious life. Such a ghost has shown his power through his appearance. The fellah makes vows on his grave, to be redeemed in his sanctuary, and that is where the votive offerings are displayed. Again and again, illness brings him to the shaykh's shrine. For illness comes from God, and not uncommonly from God through a shaykh, and so the best way to deal with it is by turning to a shaykh who is close to God and who derives his power from God. Some spirits of the dead or ghosts are more famous than others, and then people come from a long distance to seek the blessings of the place. But it often happens that such holiness loses its luster, while other shaykhs rise up and are more powerful. Then the shrine becomes dilapidated, and no one cares any more about the place where once men brought hopes and requests, where offerings were brought, and the promised sacrificial animal was slaughtered. Among these places of worship of variable life spans stand out a few shrines of ancient fame, whether their origin is from a ghost who revealed himself as particularly powerful and durable, or whether it is the last resting place of a very pious man from a somewhat mythic past who never revealed himself through a medium. As a rule very holy people never reveal themselves by descending on a person, for they are already too far from the human sphere— they are constantly with God. And in such well-known places, prayer spaces are laid out and schools are founded. People prefer to hold the Sufi *zikrs* here, ceremonies in which, constantly repeating the praise of God, people seek through abandonment of the will and discipline of the body to leave the everyday behind and to attain the sphere of the divine—God.

Legends have been woven around many of these holy men, especially the greatest of them, in the popular memory. Let us examine the different kinds of shaykh, and listen to the stories of miracles.

We begin with the fools. Certainly not every fool (*mukhabbal*, a simple-minded, confused person) is a shaykh. Only when miracles, signs of blessing, *karama* (pl. *karamat*) become visible can one know this. A sign of blessing, for example, is when the hand with which a fool was hit swells up, or if after the death of a fool people observe shining lights at the site of his death, or at his grave. In Kiman there are two people who are *mukhabbal* but are not considered shaykhs. One of them was healthy, married, and had children. Then he became *mukhabbal* so that he was no longer good for anything. His mother has to do everything for him, feed him, clean his nose. His nose is always runny, and spittle drips from his mouth. He has been like this for ten years. People would be happy if he died. The other *mukhabbal* is Kuddama. His real name is Sahhad. His father was a warder in a prison who tortured the prisoners. In those days the prisoners were not chained up in irons, but were kept in stocks. He would tighten the stocks cruelly on their hands. If they gave him money, then he relaxed the stocks. Anyone unable to give him money would be tortured. People say that because of the prayers (du'a) of the sufferers against this warder, this son was born to him. I saw this son. He would beg from people. He was a changeling or monster of about fifty. His face is of a horrifying, actually demonic, ugliness, his voice also frightening, a dry falsetto. This man was certainly not a shaykh.

A fool who is a shaykh does not beg. This is a diagnostic trait. People give them presents of their own accord.

The fool Mutwalli is a shaykh. He is a large fellow with a gray moustache. He addresses everyone as ya Muhammad—"Muhammad." With a special, cheerful yet painfully piercing look he stares into people's eyes. If you offer him a few pennies, he will only accept the coins with a hole in the middle (one-, two-, five-, and ten-millieme pieces), and even these he often gives away. He knows beforehand when someone is going to die. He then hangs around near the house of the person who might die. If you ask him, "What do you want here?" he answers softly, "So and so is going to die." Then it is not much longer until the mourning cries of the women truly ring out. Mutwalli carries the heavy bier. From the cemetery at the desert edge all the way to the village he carries the bier by himself on his shoulders, and he will not let anyone help him. This shaykh Mutwalli has already been seen in Suez and in Madina, though he has never left the area of Qift.

A girl of about twenty, Fatma, sits next to the path on the way to the market in Qift. She is lame; her two legs have hardly any musculature. In the cool of the morning someone carries her out of her miserable dwelling, where she lives with her blind mother, and places her in the sun. When the sun rises and begins to burn, the girl is carried into the shade. She is simple-minded. Her hair has been cut short to keep it clean. She speaks little and with a thick tongue, she is cheerful and smiles easily, itself a sign of a blessing, baraka. People are friendly to her because of this blessing, but they are also afraid to anger her, for perhaps this might lead to illness. The older she gets, the more the power of her baraka grows. Her prayers are very effective. Many of those who go to or from the market give her a small present and say, "Pray for me." An officer, who passes by on market days, gives her each time a silver coin and makes this request. He has seen her a couple of times in dreams and since then believes in her *baraka*. I have often observed her. Her large eyes had an unusual beauty, as if a singular incredible experience was constantly present in her soul.

Another shaykha is Labiba in Kiman. She is also *mukhabbala*. She sits in the house of her well-to-do father. If the father goes out on business, he says to her, "Pray for me—*id'ili*," and is then successful.

A very old man in Kiman told me of two holy fools from earlier times. One of these fools was named Khalil, from the Bawaba family. He used to fold his arms and smile a lot. He cursed his own clan, "*khasab ya Bawaba*—Extermination, oh Bawaba." In fact, not many members of this formerly numerous clan are now left. A contemporary of Khalil was the fool Shaykh Salim. He was an unusually fat man, and went around naked. He always greeted the other fool "a sultan Khalil."

Old Sanusi told stories of other fools. Shaykh Ahmad Mahmud lived a few years ago in Kiman. Then he left Kiman and went out into the world. He was an extremely strong lad. He could not speak properly. He used to say *hat nahma* instead of *hat lahma* for "give [me] meat." If the meat was given to him raw he would eat it raw. Sometimes he would go to people and say, "Give [me] wheat bread." And if people said, "We don't have any," while really there was a loaf there, then he would enter straight into the house, find the place where it was, and eat some of it. When children annoyed him, he would throw thick lumps of clay at them, so that they would leave him alone. At night he would sometimes climb around on the house and compound walls. Quickly and surefootedly and also backward he would climb on the high, narrow compound walls, to the horror of all who saw him. Everyone said he would fall but he never did. Once however he did fall, into the well of a waterwheel, and people thought he must have died. But he just said, "Help me out." This did not hurt him at all. In the cemetery near the tomb of Shaykh 'Ada he once saw a snake crawl into its hole. For two days he squatted in front of the hole, to catch the snake. The snake emerged two days later. The lad grabbed it with both hands. The snake bit his cheek, but he took a bite out of the snake and ate it. The snake died, but the snakebite did no harm to the lad. So he was a shaykh. This Ahmad was seen one Friday in Kiman praying in the mosque, but at the same time a man also saw him in the town of Qus. Another time he was even seen in Mecca, although he was in Kiman.

Sanusi saw another miracle man about two decades ago in Kiman, and gave him hospitality for a few days. He was a brown-skinned man with gray hair. He said he had come from the Sudan and was traveling the world. He had a long date palm rib in his hand, and at either end had added the hooves of a donkey. With this staff he was measuring the world. He said, "I have measured the world and found it equal, its breadth is like its length." Periodically he would call out, "*lehaah haah.*" He ate pebbles and would hit himself in the stomach so that you could hear the stones rattle *selolo selololo.*

Such fools taken for holy only play a small role in the religious life of the fellahin during their lifetime. If one of them was sufficiently popular, a cult might emerge at the spot of his grave. Such a cult appears most commonly when a dead person, whether or not he had been a fool in his lifetime, speaks from the beyond to living people. Such ghosts reveal themselves by entering into a living person and then announcing wishes and news through that person's mouth.

From more recent times comes, for example, the holy status of Shaykh 'Ali in Naj' al-Hijayri. He lived about two generations ago. He was *mukhabbal*, growled and grunted all kinds of natural sounds. He was married but had no children. Once he was sitting under a date palm, and while sitting threw a big stone into the crown and caused many dates to fall; no other person could have thrown a stone that high even while standing. He died as a young man during an epidemic that carried off many people. Shaykh 'Ali is rather well respected in his village.

A much more famous shaykh is Salim of Hu. Hu is north of Qena at a sharp bend in the Nile. Old Sanusi saw Salim once, when he was passing through Kiman. He was *mukhabbal*, with a heavy tongue, and grunted while laughing. He was fat beyond measure—his thighs were so wide that he had to walk with splayed-out legs. He always went around naked. One time a Christian in Kiman threw a cloth over him— a wrap of the kind women used. Then he began to cry out, "*En-nar, en-nar*" (fire, fire) and shook it off. This Salim had two brothers, who were mentally sound. When their father died, they started to divide the inheritance but began to quarrel. So the elder said, "All the possessions together make up one share, and Salim is the other share. You take

Shaykh Salim." Salim from the beginning had taken no part in the division, since he understood nothing about possessions and their values. He asked, "Have you finished dividing?" They said, "We have divided." And the younger one said, "I chose you as my share in the inheritance." So he growled like a bull, and rasped, "*Jurr*—pull [me, the bull]." The brother responded, "Your blessing [*baraka*] is enough for me." In the course of time because of this blessing the younger brother became better off than the elder one who had inherited all the possessions. Salim's tomb now stands in Hu. When the boatmen pass by they say a *Fatiha* for Shaykh Salim, to seek his blessing. It is said that many cats are kept in the sanctuary.

In Qift a few years ago lived a fisherman, Amin, from the Nasarab family. One night he went with other fishermen to a sluice to fish there without the permission of the gatekeeper. As the fishermen had their nets in the water, the gatekeeper drove his car up quietly, with no light. When he got close, he turned on the car's headlights. The fishermen jumped up and ran away. Amin fell into the water and drowned. His corpse was carried by the current close to the southern mosque in Kiman. His mother cried disconsolately. Her eyes got very inflamed. So people organized a *zar* exorcism for her, and she adorned herself with gold and silver; however, there was no *zar* in her. Then she went to a woman on whom a ghost descended at given times, possessed her, and spoke through her, predicting the future. When Amin's mother went to her, the ghost of her son himself descended on the medium. The ghost spoke, "Don't cry so much for me. It is hard for me when you cry. I sent you the eye inflammation so that you won't cry any more. If you continue to cry now, I'll make you blind." So the woman went home and stopped crying. Soon Amin's brother fell sick. They went again to the possessed woman and the ghost revealed his desire: A *qubba*, a domed sanctuary surrounded by a wall, should be built for him in the cemetery. This was done and the brother recovered.

During the Nile flood a couple of decades ago, a twelve-year-old boy named Mahmud from Kiman drowned. Soon after this loss the boy's father fell sick. He went to a person possessed by a shaykh. Also in this case the boy manifested himself in the medium and instructed his father to build him a domed tomb surrounded by a wall and to put a wooden *tabut* (pl. *tawabit*, 'honor chest') inside it.[2] Then he would get well. The father did this and recovered his health.

Yet another child from Kiman has presented himself from the world of the dead and so is considered a shaykh. He is known as Shaykh Jahlan or 'the little shaykh.' This boy fell sick when he was seven years old, and his illness lasted twenty-nine days. Some people recommended giving the sick child a glass of wine. So they went to bring some from a Copt, and the child drank it and soon died. In memory of him, his father built in the courtyard a small masonry *duwar* as a commemorative site. But soon the father fell sick, unable any longer to hold his water. He sought out a shaykh-possessed woman in Qift. The ghost of the boy himself descended on this woman and ordered the father to build him a beautiful domed tomb that would be visible from a distance, and indicated the place where he wanted it to be. When this grave monument was completed, the father regained his health. But then soon the brother of the dead boy fell sick, and they returned to the shaykh-possessed woman. The boy's ghost descended again and now asked for a *tabut* in the tomb that would be covered with a beautiful cloth. On feast days, when these *tabut*s are taken out in a procession, his should also be included. If these wishes were not fulfilled, then the brother would not get better. The wishes were fulfilled and the brother recovered.

The shrines that are created in this way are family shrines; outsiders play a very small role. However, in each village there are saints from olden times, and there is no historical memory of how they came to be. If such a shrine is beloved and frequented, then legends of miracles and magical power spring up around the saint and his place of memory.

In nearby Abnud people honor Shaykh Ghazzali, who has a beautiful domed sanctuary in the market there. He tolerates no lies. If anything is stolen, the victim says to the thief or the one he suspects of the robbery, "Come to Shaykh Ghazzali." Once inside the sanctuary the suspect must say that he did not commit the robbery. Then the victim and the

---

2 *Tabut* refers to a wooden box that covers the grave inside the memorial structure, or represents a grave located elsewhere (see p. 9). It stands about chest high, is frequently decorated or adorned, and is the focus of votive attention. NSH

suspect and others present say the *Fatiha* together. If the suspect lies, Shaykh Ghazzali will cause him to fall sick and eventually die. If the suspect swears falsely and then regrets it, he has to return the stolen object, wash his body with milk, and then go to the shrine to ask the shaykh for pardon.

In the sacred shrine of Shaykh Yusuf in Kiman, no criminal can enter; he would find his way blocked.

Shaykh 'Awayda, also known for short as 'Ada, is a respected saint. His domed grave sanctuary is in a corner of the cemetery of Qift and its villages. Today the settled Bedouin 'Azayza from the desert fringe claim him as their own. But the elders know that the grave of 'Awayda was already there when the 'Azayza came. People recounted some of his miracles. Once he started off by camel on his way to 'his country,' the Hijaz. He rode to Qusayr on the Red Sea, where he took his great flat wooden bowl, which every Bedouin household has, put it in the water, and sailed on it across the sea. He came back on the same vessel, mounted his camel, and returned to this people, the 'Azayza, on the fringe of the desert. This bowl was miraculous in other ways. When 'Awayda had guests, he would use it to serve them food. The miracle was that the bowl was never empty. Once one of the guests who didn't believe in the miracle secretly pushed one handful after another of the food into a bag. The bag filled up, but the bowl was not empty. The man was then convinced and venerated Shaykh 'Awayda.

Today when someone is robbed, he goes to the tomb of 'Awayda, asks for help, and vows, for instance, a ram as a sacrifice. Shaykh 'Awayda then works on the conscience of the thief so that he secretly returns the stolen object. But if the person robbed does not keep his vow, the shaykh afflicts him with pain and sickness. Thus he is brought to reflect on his promise, and bring his sacrifice and recover.

A man from Kiman was lining the lower part of his well shaft. Unfortunately the well sides caved in, and stones and earth fell into the bottom. People ran to this man's father and said, "Your son has passed away." However, the man in the well, seeing himself threatened, had called out to the saint, "*Ya Shaykh 'Ada*." The shaykh then lifted him up, and he was unhurt. Out of gratitude, a bull calf was slaughtered for 'Ada.

When a cow is stubborn and won't let herself be milked, she is taken to Shaykh 'Ada at midnight. Two men lead the animal. When they approach the cemetery, one of the two undresses completely and is as naked "as he was when his mother gave birth," and hands his clothes to the other. He then leads the cow on a halter behind him, without looking around and without saying a word, and circumambulates the domed tomb of 'Awayda three, five, or seven times, and always from right to left, that is, counterclockwise. Many people circumambulate not just Shaykh 'Awayda but the entire cemetery. This may have been the original way.

Southwest of Qift lies the village of al-Shaykhiya. It is said that in earlier days the place was further west, directly on the Nile. But the water began to wash against the houses so that the peasants moved away and settled where the village is now. When the water flooded the entire old village, it did not touch the site of a shaykh's grave, the shaykh Hajj 'Ali. This was a sign of the blessing (baraka) of the shaykh. So the people decided to disinter the saint's body and to take it with them. When they opened the grave, they found that the body had not decayed, even though it had been there for a very long time. This was a new demonstration of his power to bless. The people brought new clothes for the corpse and buried it in the new village near the mosque and built a shrine over it. Then later on when once the ship of a pasha was traveling on the Nile, and reached the level of old al-Shaykhiya, it could not continue but instead began to turn in circles. The pasha suspected immediately that this was the doing of a saint, and began to investigate. Then the people of al-Shaykhiya dug once more next to the grave of Hajj 'Ali and found the equally pristine body of the saint's daughter. They took it and reburied it in new al-Shaykhiya next to her father. Time went by, and the veneration for the saint and his holy daughter became subject to doubt. People used to illuminate the shrine on certain days. But they were puzzled because the refilled oil lamps did not last but soon went out. Then they discovered that a fox was sneaking into the shrine and licking the oil from the lamp. So the people got angry at the shaykh (who let the fox do this) and many began to despise him. But when the fox came one more time to lick up the oil, he stayed there hanging by his tongue as in a trap. They found him caught like this when they came in the morning. They beat him to death. Thus the shaykh proved the strength of his miracles once more and was henceforth again highly venerated. The shrines of many shaykhs, including this one, are entrusted to the special care of a person. Such a caretaker is called *naqib* (fem. *naqiba*, pl. *nuqaba*). The father of the present caretaker held this post. The saint's blessing revealed itself through him. When he died, like any other, he was laid out in the mosque so that the funeral prayer could be performed. Then when people wanted to lift the bier to their shoulders to carry him to the cemetery, they could not move the corpse from the spot. Thereupon the gathering recited the *Fatiha*. That worked, and they were able to lift the bier to their shoulders and walk to the cemetery. However, then it turned out to be impossible to put the dead body down. He obliged the bearers to return to the village, to circle the shrine of Hajj 'Ali seven times, then he finally let them put him down before the door of the shrine. Now there was no more moving him from there, so he was buried in the anteroom of the shrine. A *tabut* was also provided for him.

This anteroom is the place where the animals dedicated for sacrifice to the shaykh are brought. The tools needed for this are kept there—two knives, two huge cooking pots, a wooden ladle, a double hook to hang up the slaughtered animal (for skinning and butchering), and a wooden scale with scale pans made from plaited date fronds. Most of all, you can see here the famous oil lamp, an old, rusty lamp closed on top. It is impossible to lick oil out of it—the fox would have had to drink from it as from a bottle. But this doesn't bother anyone. Here also are hanging various votive offerings and scraps of cloth and knotted rags from women who were hoping for a husband or children through the saint's *baraka*.

Near the house where I lived in Kiman two completely ruined shrines stood on a pile of ruins. One of these belonged to Shaykh Abu Shahba, the other to Shaykh 'Ubaydallah.

Abu Shahba is a shaykh from olden times who is supposed to have come from the East. An aged man in Kiman told me the following story. Once the floodwaters came so close to his house that they threatened to damage it. So he took his fellah's hoe, and went to the raised little shrine of Abu Shahba to fetch earth to make a dike. However, people warned him. But he laughed at them, and said, "What does this shaykh mean to me?" He began to cut loose clods of earth, but the hoe jumped out of his land and leaped at his leg on its own. His people fetched him and he had to remain at home in bed for fifteen days. When he was lying on his sick bed, a powerful dragon came,[3] opened his jaws, and took his head between his teeth and held him up with his legs in the air. Then the dragon turned into a young, male camel, who bellowed in the manner of a camel and tried to trample him underfoot. The man realized that all this came from the insulted Shaykh Abu Shahba. As soon as he could move again, he went to the shaykh's shrine, took off his shoes, and held them with the soles on his headband as a sign of his humility, and said, "I regret it." Thereupon things improved for him quickly. He vowed to the very well-known Sidi 'Abd al-Rahim of Qena that he would visit him on his birthday when he was completely cured. He recovered and visited this saint.

Earlier Abu Shahba was well respected. His shrine had a caretaker who had the beautiful name of Bakhit al-Zarrat. There was an annual festival for Abu Shahba, with a *layla*, a 'night.' Once at this nighttime festival it happened that a rider knocked over a girl and the horse mortally wounded the girl. Bakhit took the girl and buried her. With this accident, the festival came to an end, and in the following years it was never again celebrated.

The neighbor of this saint is Shaykh 'Ubaydallah, of whose shrine only the foundation walls are still standing. And yet he had also once performed a great miracle. A man vowed a ram to 'Ubaydallah if he would restore his son to health. The child recovered, and the father prepared the ram for the sacrifice. But then the ram was stolen. The man searched everywhere, but to no avail. Finally he went to a neighbor, who he thought was the thief, and asked him, "Is the ram here?" The neighbor said, "No," but in fact he had stolen the ram and had already slaughtered it and put it in the cooking pot. Suddenly there arose from the pot a voice: "*bah bah*." So the thief was trapped. That the piece of meat could bleat came from the blessing power (*baraka*) of Shaykh 'Ubaydallah. Another time a man brought Shaykh 'Ubaydallah a ram as a sacrifice for the shrine. He pinched the *naqiba*, or caretaker, in the bottom. She was furious and said, "Are you visiting me or the shaykh?"

---

3 When a snake *ta'bun* is fully grown, it acquires wings, and becomes an *af* (pl. *ifan*). And as such it flies to Sidi Ahmad al-Rifa'i in the wastelands, *ard al-kharab*. HAW

She threw the meat on the ground, and chased away the festive group, already assembled, including drummers and pipers.

These various shaykhs can be considered as family or village saints. Their circle of veneration is quite small, the lifetime of their cult is in general limited to a couple of generations; in rare cases the cult maintains its special form for a couple of centuries. These shaykhs are close to human society, and some reveal themselves at times through a medium. At a higher level than the family and village saints are a few long-established town saints. Their circle of veneration is much larger, their cult is more lively and long-lasting. They are enthroned higher in the world of spirits than the other saints, and thus they do not descend in order to speak to people through a medium.

Shaykh Ansari, usually called Nusari, is one of this type. He has a beautiful sanctuary in Qift; a clean courtyard for prayer and *zikr*s is next to the domed shrine, all enclosed by a high wall and shaded by trees. Ansari was in a holy war somewhere in a field far away. He was fighting in a battle against the unbelievers, and his head was sliced off. Then came the miracle: He held the separated head in both hands on his neck and roared through the air 'like an airplane.' He finally landed here in Qift and died. The people buried him and built him a shrine.

The other major shaykh who is highly venerated in Qift is Hamil al-Raya, literally 'the standard-bearer.' He too fought in holy wars and attacked the ranks of the enemy with the red banner in his hand. People say he was one of the companions of the Prophet Muhammad, but they also say that this saint came from the nearby town of Qus. Hamil al-Raya was wounded in battle and died near Qift. The people buried him and built a shrine. Many years ago the shrine had to be renovated, so the grave was dug up and people soon noticed a wonderful heavenly odor. They found that the corpse was completely without decay. Next to the saint the corpse of his brother was likewise undecayed. A piece of paper was found under the saint's head where one could read when the standard-bearer came to Qift. This was more than a thousand years ago.

The regional saint, Sidi 'Abd al-Rahim of Qena, is enthroned even higher than these town saints in the world of saints.

At about the same level the members of brotherhoods rank their founders. Much venerated in Naj' al-Hijayri and Kiman is Sidi Muhammad al-Dandarawi. He is said to have died thirty-six years ago.

Dandarawi served, voluntarily and without pay, the great shaykh and founder of a brotherhood, Ibrahim al-Rashidi. He was a water-carrier and with his water skin he looked after Rashidi's guests. He served in this way until he grew old. Once he fell on the stairs while carrying the water skin. The dervishes said to Rashidi, "Dandarawi fell on the steps." The shaykh went there and asked him, "Have you reached the goal?" Dandawari answered, "God brought me to the goal," namely to the end of his lengthy service. Rashidi then said, "Your time of service is finished." He made him into a shaykh and his deputy. After the death of Rashidi he took over the leadership of the brotherhood (tariqa, the 'way').

Old Sanusi saw Dandarawi in the house of his pious father. Dandarawi was a very tall, thin, white-haired man, who spoke sparingly. Once he sat during the Friday prayers at home, yet at the same time he was seen in the mosque.

Khedive 'Abbas invited him to visit, and said, "Will you take me on?" Dandarawi remained mute and looked straight ahead, as if lost in meditation. The khedive was concerned and after a while asked again, "Will you take me on?" Then Dandarawi spoke, "I'll speak later. Leave me alone for now. In such and such a place, a friend of mine has died." The khedive had a telegram sent immediately: "Did such and such a man die there and is Dandarawi there?" Then came the answer, which certified that the man in question had died and that Dandarawi was among the mourners.

Dandarawi had a daughter who was married in Syria, a son Abul 'Abbas, and a younger son 'Abd al-Wahhab. The daughter did not know Abul 'Abbas. When Dandarawi once visited his daughter in Syria, she said to him, "Who will be your successor?" Dandarawi said, "Abul 'Abbas, you will recognize him." Dandarawi traveled further and died. Abul 'Abbas took over the leadership of the brotherhood. Once he traveled to Syria to see his sister. He found her and before he could say who he was, she shouted with joy, "Hiya hiya hiya Abul 'Abbas hiya hiya." So they organized a big celebration. Many people asked Abul 'Abbas to take them into the brotherhood, and he accepted many of them.

People recount many miracles of Dandarawi. In Mecca or in Madina, Dandarawi had a servant and a girl who was married to him. She committed a terrible misdeed. The servant went to his master, Dandarawi, and told him the story and asked him to whip her. Dandarawi said, "It is better for her to die." He uncovered his head and prayed against her to God, so that the woman would die. From this hour on the woman felt she was being strangled: "God strangled her." She groaned and two days later she was dead.

Once people wanted to test Dandarawi to see if he was really such a miracle worker. A man lay on the funeral bier, in pretense. People told Dandarawi to pray the prayer of the dead for him. He answered, "Remove the man." They pressured him, and repeated, "Pray the prayer of the dead." So he did. Then the people removed the shroud and he was dead.

Already twenty years before his death, Dandarawi predicted there would be a king in Egypt, and moreover, that a railroad linking Qift and Qusayr would be built.

Once a man was praying behind Dandarawi, who was acting as prayer leader, and he had tied up a piece of meat in the end of his scarf. After the prayer the man went home and wanted to cook the meat. It stayed in the pot and the water boiled and bubbled but the meat didn't cook, staying as raw and red as when it was bought. The man built up the fire and cooked it for a long time but it did not change. So he went to Dandarawi and told him the story. Dandarawi said, "The meat was behind me in prayer, and fire has no power over anything that was behind me in prayer." So the people knew that they did not need to fear the fires of hell as long as they prayed behind Dandarawi.

The Image of the World and Islam

The spatial world image is essentially limited to the narrow strip of the Nile Valley, including the home village of the Upper Egyptian fellah. To the east and west stand the hills of the desert. The desert is alien and forbidding to him, and since he cannot cultivate it he is indifferent to it. Thus his world image is limited. To the north he knows Cairo, and knows that he can travel north for several days and remain between the desert hills and the fruitful Egyptian fields. The north is familiar to him. Many peasants have traveled to Cairo, and some to the sea at Alexandria. The south is different. There is only a short stretch in which he would find Egyptian peasants at work. He knows that then come the lands of the dark-skinned Africans, different from him in appearance, language, and customs. In his thinking he situates in this mythical south all the stories people tell about the marvelous, the adventurous, and the fabulous.

The south is, so to speak, the gap in his otherwise sharply contained world image. For instance, in the south the women practice magic. If an Egyptian marries a woman there, and does not want to remain always with her, she will change him into an animal, a dog, a donkey, a hyena, whatever she wants. When the man is at home, the woman lets him be a man, but if he leaves she will transform him into an animal. So he stays as a matter of course.

Closer to him than this dangerous human world in the south is the underground spirit world. Sometimes the underground spirits allow themselves to be felt nearby. In the time of the Prophet Muhammad, Imam 'Ali descended, on God's orders, to the world beneath us, to the *jinn* there. He fought with them. Then the Companions said to the Prophet Muhammad, "The imam has gone to the *jinn*." So the Prophet of God went to the hole through which the imam had descended, and called to him. He answered, "Very good, very good. I am alive, and fighting the *jinn*." Thus the Prophet and the others knew that he was in good health. Later the imam climbed back up to earth.

A sense of time depth is equally missing from the world image. The decisive event in all the course of time is the appearance of the Prophet Muhammad. But this event is not fixed by actual years inside a history of humanity that has lasted centuries, since the fellah counts neither years nor centuries. The concept of history has no place in his head, so therefore he cannot see Muhammad as a historical appearance. Muhammad is close enough to have lived yesterday, and distant enough so that the world began with him. Even the real and legendary happenings of the early days of Islam, which recur frequently in songs, are not strung together in a historical sequence. The death of the Prophet and that of his grandson Husayn occurred almost half a century apart. According to legend, however, the Prophet experienced the death of Husayn. It is told that, as Husayn was killed in battle and cut into pieces, his horse returned alone. The Prophet said, "His body is coming." Then the individual body parts, cut into pieces, came to the Prophet—the storyteller indicated with his hand a low zigzag-shaped pile on the ground. These parts were assembled and buried.

Present-day humanity can be divided into Muslims, Christians, and heathens. Christians and heathens count as candidates for hell. Muslims can be divided into four schools of interpretation, but then there is also a fifth school. This one is abominable. Followers of this school live in Persia. The traditions of these people stipulate that one should urinate on the holy black stone in Mecca, *al-hijra al-nabawiya*. When these people go on pilgrimage to Mecca, and want to follow this shameful commandment, the righteous Muslims fight them until blood flows, not with sticks, but with the soles of their shoes. Someone who belongs to this fifth school is called *khamsi*. *Khamsi* is thus a weighty curse word for Upper Egyptian peasants.

Just as the view of the past is dominated by the image of the Prophet, so the view of the future is caught up in the imagery of the Day of Judgment. The end of the world and the last judgment will be foretold by various signs. Among these is the appearance of the Antichrist, the Dajjal. He is beneath the earth and will come out from there when the end is nigh. Some people say that the Dajjal will emerge in a village named Humr between al-Shaykhiya and Qus. The people of Humr do not otherwise have a bad reputation. Other people say that the Dajjal will come forth from Qus and more precisely from the lane of the pigeon-dung dealers. Also many believe the Mahdi will appear before the end of the world. Abul 'Abbas, the son of Dandarawi, could soon reveal himself as the Mahdi.

On the day of resurrection all people will shoot up from their coccyges like plants from their seed. Then all the resurrected must cross the bridge to the Hereafter; for the pious believers this bridge is as wide as a desert valley and for the evildoers as narrow as a hair. The bridge is 'the doubled-bladed sword of God' *(sayf Allah bihaddin)*.

We have seen that in the everyday needs of the fellahin, ghosts play an important role as cause and as helper. This will be made even clearer in this book. But it is of decisive importance that behind the world of the ghosts, through Islam, the depth of an eternal meaning and the eternal as goal are opened up. Many fellahin may make vows to shaykhs, bring sacrifices to tombs, say their prayers nearby, but the prayer itself is directed to the Lord of the Worlds. This stormy breakthrough of all barriers of the world surrounded by spirits is expressed in the mystical devotional exercises of the brotherhoods—the *zikr*. I observed such exercises many times. They made a deep impression on me. Here I present two accounts, just as I wrote them in my diary immediately after the event.

To honor Shaykh ʻAli in Najʻ al-Hijayri—this simpleton who could throw a stone into the crown of a date palm while seated—his brother Hajj Ismaʻin organized a *zikr*. He had vowed to do this in a moment of need.

It took place on February 28, 1934, about 9 p.m. As I was about to go to bed, there was a knock: A man from Najʻ al-Hijayri came to say that there was a *zikr* this night in this village, as had been vowed by Hajj Ismaʻin. I set off immediately. The full moon beautifully lit up the silent fields. From the area of the cemeteries came a strange song, to which we listened with gaping mouths; it was only a waterwheel. We reached Najʻ al-Hijayri. Houses and walls glistened in white surfaces. The tamarisks from a garden threw their shadows wide over the path. Now the muffled sound of the stamping steps of the *zikr* dancers came to us from nearby. The messenger of Hajj Ismaʻin came to meet us in the street. He led me through the low door into Hajj Ismaʻin's house. Next to the entrance on the right is a small room. The dignified master of the place *(sahib al-mahall)*, the pilgrim Ismaʻin, sat there, a white-bearded man with a well-kept appearance. We used to imagine such figures in the stories of Harun al-Rashid. He was squatting before a clay charcoal brazier, warming his hands. The floor was covered with mats. A small petroleum lamp sat in a niche on the wall. I was supposed to sit next to him, but the *zikr* brothers were in the room to the left of the entrance so I went there. Two women were standing in the corridor and peeking at the dancers. They ducked to the side when I came, and discreetly pulled their headscarves in front of their faces, and looked only through a slit with curiously shining eyes at the second event of the evening, the European stranger. Someone brought a wobbly chair, and leaned it against the wall, and I sat down. From a high niche came the light of the kerosene lamp into the dust-filled room. A dozen young men stood next to the wall under the lamp. They were stamping their feet, swinging their torsos forward and backward, and breathing out the name of God—*Allah*. Facing them, on the wall, a second row was standing: These were young lads, ranging from twelve to sixteen years old, and in the most distant corner was a group of boys, seven, eight, and ten years old. They were also eagerly swinging their bodies, while the youngest of them were tired out, squatting in the corner, sleeping. In the middle between the two rows was the leader, Sulayman, the "choir-master," *munshid* (pl. *munshidin*). He was from Bir 'Anbar, situated on the desert road to Qena, but he was not a Bedouin. He was a stocky, muscular man, in his late twenties, and had a brown face with a black moustache. He was wearing a dark blue robe. He held his left hand to his ear in order to hear the resonance of his own voice, which was now loud and clear. He rocked his body back and forth, and also nodded his head. The expression on his face was almost savage. He was no longer a subject, not a man who sings, but a man who had become song. The swaying of his body and head and the rhythmical music found expression in his lithe body. Here there was no melody, what to our ears would be a solid harmonic sequence of sounds. Nevertheless there were different manners. And with each manner the men's dance changed. Giving oneself over to the music, the submission of the *munshid* led to a very remarkable fashioning of the sounds. Sometimes he made an effort in a rather deep pitch to shape the words in the back of the throat, and in this way to nasalize them. A dreadful kind of gurgling was what came out, and that apparently especially stimulated the dancers. It seemed to me as if his total devotion to the singing brought out the deep involvement of the others in this dance. Sometimes he started out with the song, meanwhile the bodies continued to sway, holding to the rhythm or determining a new one. Then he began to clap his hands softly to the beat, as soft as the beating of the wings of bats, which occasionally dart through the dust-filled air. This stimulated in quite a different way. At this invitation the dancers fell silent, who had until now accompanied their movement and the song of the *munshid* with "*Allahh Allahh.*" Now they swung their bodies lightly to the left and strongly to the right and began to murmur the name of God—*Allah*. But this is no more a word that they whispered, but three puffs of breath, in two short and frightful puffs they breathed in *h – h*, then in a long gasp they breathed out, *h*. The *munshid* now began to add to his soft clapping low and ingratiating singing—"*ya Dandarawi,*" I heard again and again. His song picked up speed, he himself became more ecstatic, the movements of the dancers became more pronounced, more extreme, their regular breathing turned to panting. The *munshid* abandoned all words, he sang, "*den den den den . . . .*" There was a sound as when one taps with the finger on the edge of a hand drum, he sang "*dil dil dil dil . . .* as when one picks at a string. He formed words again—

"ya Dandarawi, ya Dandarawi"—as usual he slurred the sound, like the crazy music of the Egyptian reed pipe *zummara*. All of a sudden he stopped, and at the same time the dancers stopped swinging their bodies and forcing their breathing. Not one continued to sway. One used the end of his headdress to wipe the sweat from his brow. The brothers squatted down. In an instant the *munshid* began to fill the break with his song. I think he was improvising. He sang of Dandarawi, of the Lord God, of the Prophet Muhammad, of paradise. The brothers were all looking at him: They were full of excitement, content with his words, and called out something like *"ma'lum"* (that's right), when he sang how marvelous paradise is and how it is sure that every Muslim will go there. He sang *"ya 'ayni*—Oh my eye, my darling," and meant by that the Prophet Muhammad, and extended the *i* for so long that his face turned dark and the veins swelled up. The brothers enthusiastically responded to the performance with *"Allah Allah."*

I distinguished on the whole the following dance types: The brothers stand close together, they give themselves over to the dance with limp torso and head—all headscarves loose—and begin to sway weakly to the left and strongly to the right, however, with a quarter-turn, and they speak or breathe *Allahh* and *h-h-h*. The same exercise they make with a half turn of the body, or kneeling, one knee is raised, the body makes quarter turns. Or the brothers stand up straight, and let their body lean forward, very much to the front, and not so far to the back, and stamp with their feet. The most remarkable impression is that of the total abandonment and devotion of the participants. It is also worth noticing the feeling for rhythm that they have. If the *munshid* stops, instantly they all stop; if he switches into another beat they quickly follow. They bring themselves to the edge of frenzy, but never go beyond it. One, who was moving his body with exceptional eagerness, occasionally cried out during the *munshid*'s song *"Allah Allah Allah."* His voice sounded like the sweet sorrow of ecstasy. Another occasionally clapped his hands to the rhythm, so much was he himself rhythm and measure that merely rocking his body and calling out were no longer enough. The *munshid* was accompanied in many of his songs by a chorus of three to six men and boys who stood near him.

After I had been watching this ardent religious performance for about two hours, the singer stopped for a long pause. He pulled a cover

over his heated head and shoulders and instructed a boy, dressed in white, who had been standing next to him the whole time, to sing. I had already noticed this youth. He was about fourteen years old. He came from the ʿAbabda, from their village on the desert fringe south of Najʿ al-Hijayri. He had an appealing soft child's face. He was blind; I could only see his profile. He began to sing in a pleasing gentle voice. He sang the praises of the Lord God, only *"ya rabb"* (O Lord), this *rabb* over many tones, rising and falling, rising and falling, and rising drawn out. The boy's face was smiling, happy to be singing, happy to be singing of God. All could feel the pure heart of this youth. The brothers straightened themselves up and looked with wide eyes at the youth, calling out enthusiastically. And the youth continued to sing. The glow of the kerosene lantern reflected off his unseeing eyes and white teeth. He sang of the Lord God, he sang from the Qur'an, he sang of Muhammad. Occasionally he would lead the song into the *zikr* rhythm and clap his hands softly. When one of his songs came to an end, the meaning of his song intensified to the thought and word, Lord God, he raised his right index finger and with his hand led the music to its paroxysm, and pointed to heaven. . . . I left. The brothers sat for a while together, ate a few dates, then went to sleep in high hopes of the garden of God.

The *zikr* of the Dandarawi devotees in Najʿ al-Hijayri followed the pattern of the Ahmadiya brothers. On another occasion I attended the *zikr* of the Shazliya brothers. The simple-minded and crippled Fatma, who used to sit on the path to the Qift market every single day, had only one brother, who looked after her and her blind mother. His name was ʿAbbas. This ʿAbbas used to take his donkey to the desert in order to bring back saltpeter for fertilizer. Once when he returned he was very disturbed, threw a nonsensical fit, and cried despairingly. People took this to mean that the ghost of a dead person had seized him. The local government doctor sent him outside the town to the quarantine precinct, where a number of sick people were kept. I saw ʿAbbas there, a pathetic sight, his face contorted in inexpressible misery, frothing from the corners of his mouth, and on his lips a paste of bread and soil. In his fists he offered me clumps of bread squeezed together. He could no longer speak correctly. From time to time his body became taut, and the expression on his face grew determined and angry, then he would scream "Mahmud, Mahmud." People said that this Mahmud he was calling was a shaykh, the ghost of a dead person, the one who must have seized him in the desert. People tried everything to bring him to his senses, but they were happy first of all when the government doctor released him.

I will have more to say about 'Abbas later; now is the time to describe the *zikr* that was introduced in the context of this customary treatment. People believed that the ghost of the deceased Mahmud had sought out 'Abbas as a medium, so that in the future he could expect to come down regularly on him. The *zikr*, held next to the sanctuary of Shaykh Ansari in Qift, was intended to establish peaceful relations between 'Abbas and the ghost. People regarded 'Abbas as someone dedicated to the shaykh, a man whose future life would be given over to mediating between the dead and the living, who would have no individual participation in people's daily lives, who would not be able to marry and have children. I was invited to this *zikr* by relatives of 'Abbas. As I was on my way to this evening event, and was walking slowly through the moonlit ruins of Koptos and was taking pleasure in the fleecy clouds, I could hear gunshots, drumbeats, and singing coming from a nearby village. It was a marriage. I went there. A large group of men in beautiful festive robes was parading through the lanes, many carrying candles in their hands, and one was swinging a kerosene lantern. The groom strode in festive dress in the midst of his friends, a white silk shawl around his shoulders. People were continually singing the song of the groom—"The rose was but a thorn, it opened thanks to the sweat of the Prophet"; two men most of all, perhaps a brother and an uncle of the groom, could not sing it often enough, and looked at the groom with radiant faces, as if they were bringing him a new and lovely message. People were as happy as children. Sometimes the procession stopped altogether; in any case it advanced only slowly. Then the comrades picked someone from among them and lifted him up with their combined strength. However, the groom was not part of this. The groom walked seriously and full of solemn joy—as if he felt that in the ever-repeated meeting of man and wife now the first meeting of the two halves of the cosmos would be reenacted. He was carrying this cosmic load.

From this marriage I went to 'Abbas whom a ghost had selected and thus taken from him the desire for a wife. Next to the grave of Shaykh Ansari the covered place was ready for a celebration. Mats had been spread and lamps on the walls threw off light. The brothers sat there in a semicircle; 'Abbas was among them wearing a white robe. In front of the brother, in the center, sat a shaykh with a long beard, who led the exercises. The shaykh sang in a dignified and solemn way, as if in a mass. The brothers recited "*Allah Allah*." The shaykh's right hand gave signs to increase and decrease the tempo; he was holding his hand palm downward. The brothers recited "*Allah Allah*" more quickly, then rose, brought themselves together in a circle and said "*hu hu*"—He, He (God)—and bowed the upper part of the body forward. Faster and faster came the beat, *ho ho ho*. The brothers were holding each other's hands. Then they all sat down in a circle; the shaykh sang with a full voice and melodiously the praise names of God. The brothers responded with a refrain. 'Abbas did his best to perform along with them. When the song leader and the chorus were silent, one could hear his heavy breathing. Often this breathing sounded convulsive as if after much weeping. The *zikr* lasted late into the night. 'Abbas's relatives brought tea for the guests. Everyone agreed that 'Abbas was doing better now. But he was worn out, sitting alone, and staring at a wall.

PART TWO

'Abd al-Radi

'Abd al-Radi's Origins

I recall my first meeting with 'Abd al-Radi. In early December 1933 I came for the second time to Kiman and settled at Sanusi's house. I heard that in the neighboring village of Naj' al-Hijayri, about half a year previously, a man had been possessed by a shaykh, the ghost of his uncle Bakhit, and that this ghost/spirit knew how to give miraculous information. I went with my assistant, Mahdi, the oldest son of Sanusi, over to the nearby Naj' al-Hijayri. Close to the western edge of the village stood 'Abd al-Radi's house; next to it there was the steep white-washed dome of a shrine; in front of it in a tiny courtyard there was a sycamore seedling; in front of that, in the street, a watering trough for passing cows, and a drinking water fountain for people. An old man was squatting in front of the house, and he jumped up in surprise when we asked for 'Abd al-Radi. This was his father. He said his son would come soon: He had gone to the mosque for the afternoon prayer. I sat down. After a while a couple of men came. One of them struck me immediately by his pale face and his shy, pensive look. On his fore-head he still had the light dust mark from the prayer, the prostration before God, in the mosque. Mahdi said, "That is the shaykh." I greeted him. We sat down together, surrounded by relatives and neighbors, and spoke of farmers and farm work, of faraway Germany, of the war. But soon 'Abd al-Radi led me through the low doorway into the interior of the farmhouse. There we were alone, just his father and my assistant Mahdi were still there. 'Abd al-Radi asked me, "Did you come for the shaykh, shall he descend?" I said, "If it is possible let him come down." 'Abd al-Radi said, "This is not one of the days when the shaykh comes, but perhaps he will come for your sake." He led me through a door into a small yard immediately adjacent to his living area. There was a corner here with mats laid out and covered by a thatched roof. This was the *khilwa*. Here 'Abd al-Radi used to sit when he was expecting the ghost and here the advice seekers sit around him. Because the descent of the ghost is by the grace of God, so this *khilwa* is also a sacred place, and we had to remove our shoes—all those who sit here, just as in a mosque. 'Abd al-Radi sat leaning against the wall and asked his younger brother to prepare the incense pot. In a few moments he brought the round vessel.

I waited in the greatest excitement for the "descent of the shaykh, the spirit of the dead." Anyone who wants information from the shaykh must give his medium, in this case 'Abd al-Radi, while he is possessed, a token—*riha* (pl. *riyah*, 'smell')—from the person about whom he wishes the information. Thus someone wishing counsel on a child's sickness should bring the child's cap, or to heal a cow, some hairs from the cow's tail, or to find out news from a distant person, something belonging to that person. He should put this in the hand of the one possessed. If one wants information about one's own affairs, one should offer a handkerchief, a cap, a waistband, or simply extend one's own hand. One should include a small gift of money with this token. I had wrapped up a couple of pennies in my handkerchief, and hoped to hear news from my relatives, or at least about my family. 'Abd al-Radi sat there quietly and with half-closed eyes, from time to time he rocked from side to side. He tossed a few grains of incense in the embers, and a thin wispy smoke arose. The smoke must have entered his nose. He rose quickly from a squatting to a kneeling position,[4] grabbed the incense pot, brought it to his mouth and inhaled the smoke greedily, gulping down mouthfuls. Then he tossed the pot casually onto the mat, where old

---

4 Here as elsewhere, 'squatting' refers to a posture where a person 'sits on his heels,' that is, with the feet flat on the ground and the thighs on the heels. NSH

Hamed, his father, caught it and set it upright. 'Abd al-Radi was now really someone else altogether. His posture was erect and full of energy. However, his mouth muscles seemed completely lax, his breathing was heavy and quick, his tongue gurgled at the intake of breath, his lips were listless and were spraying saliva while he breathed out. His eyes clouded over. He spoke loudly and in fits and starts. First he uttered a couple of religious expressions—the words were distorted, the sounds themselves in part simplified. The possessed one held out his hand to me. I gave him my handkerchief. He unwrapped the coins and slipped them under the mat behind him. He squeezed and twisted my handkerchief a little in his hand. Then he spoke laboriously and gestured. He then vaguely predicted an upcoming trip—"*pff pff pff,*" he said to indicate a train, pointed southward with his hand, and clapped his hands together twice. This meant that the trip would take place in twenty days, according to the interpretation of old Hamed. During all this, the possessed one sometimes laughed very unpleasantly. He indicated that I have children, and with his hand showed that one is big, the other smaller. Using two fingers he indicated two children. Then he said, "wife," raised both hands to his face and indicated the long hair of the "wife," and stroked his robe to show her fine clothing. "All are well," he said. The children are playing ball and flute, he announced through words and gestures. Suddenly he sank down completely, and fell back so that his back and head hit the wall behind him. He then came to himself, and his eyes again took on life. With a soft and unsure voice he greeted us, "*marhaba,*" welcome. After a brief pause, he asked whether Shaykh Bakhit had said anything to make us angry. No, we said. 'Abd al-Radi appeared to be exhausted. The contrast between the soft voice and the limp body now, with the loud voice and the taut body earlier, was striking.

I was able to study 'Abd al-Radi for about four months, taking part in innumerable sessions, winning over his trust, and trying to understand him and to discern the effect of this on the fellahin.

On his father's side, 'Abd al-Radi comes from the large family of the Nasarab, on his mother's from the Atwal family. Both families claim an Arab origin, they are sure of it, even though today they are thoroughly mixed with Upper Egyptian fellah blood. Here is 'Abd al-Radi's family tree:

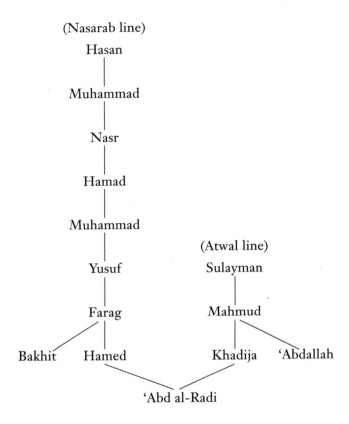

(Nasarab line)
Hasan

Muhammad

Nasr

Hamad

Muhammad

Yusuf   (Atwal line)
           Sulayman

Farag   Mahmud

Bakhit   Hamed   Khadija   'Abdallah

'Abd al-Radi

'Abd al-Radi is the eldest son of his father and mother. He has five younger brothers. His father is a man of sixty to seventy. He maintains that he is 110 years old. When the fellahin give their ages, they want to pass themselves off as in their forties for as long as possible, but when it is obvious that this time has passed by, they prefer to present themselves as an ancient patriarch. The mother of 'Abd al-Radi is a small blind woman of fifty to sixty.

It is important that both in the paternal and in the maternal families of 'Abd al-Radi spiritual abnormalities have appeared.

The most important is Bakhit, 'Abd al-Radi's father's brother. This Bakhit died in fact more than thirty years ago. 'Abd al-Radi never knew him. He was *mukhabbal* (simple-minded). His face was not like other people's. His spittle ran over his lips and dripped down to his chin. He often worked his mouth like a camel, *pu pu pu pu pu*. He was an insatiable eater and very fat. He was no use at work. If he worked at anything it turned out poorly. He spoke little and didn't laugh at all. He often wandered around in the neighboring villages. He spent many nights outside in the lanes and fields, and he liked to roam in the lonely desert. He addressed all men in the same way, by the name Muhammad. His speech was often peculiar. People still recalled some of his own construction of words—thus he called the village Barahma always Barahmama, and the village al-Shaykhiya always Ashiya. A woman named Miska he called Samaka. As a boy he once stole some pomegranates from the garden of his uncle (father's brother) Hasan, and gave them to children. The uncle beat him for this. But then the hand which he had used swelled up. Thus he knew that Bakhit was a shaykh, a holy man. He said to him, "*sammihni*" (be good to me, forgive me). Bakhit answered, "I am good to you." Then his hand was cured. Another time his brother Hamed hit him because he was angry about Bakhit's gluttony—"All you can do is eat, constantly eat," he said. Bakhit then wept, went out, and wandered about for a few days in the neighboring villages. But Hamed's hand also swelled up because of the blessing power *(baraka)* of Bakhit.

Bakhit must have been in his twenties. Once he was, as usual, moving around. At nightfall he was in the village of Kharishiya near Abnud in the house of the local mayor, whose name was Mellah. Bakhit had not shown any signs of special illness in those days, but unexpectedly he died in the house of this mayor. The mayor was in those days rather poor, but he insisted on providing the shroud for Bakhit, who was staying with him when he died, and on taking care of the burial, even though Hamed came quickly to the village when he heard the news of Bakhit's death, and brought a shroud with him. But Mellah did not accept that, and also insisted on covering the costs of the interment. Bakhit repaid him. Mellah's business went much better after that, and he became rich in goods and honor. Bakhit was buried in the Abnud cemetery. In his memory, for he had become a shaykh, Hamed built a low circular wall *(duwar)* next to his house.

The ghost of this Bakhit is now the one who has possessed 'Abd al-Radi and speaks through his mouth to people.

On his father's side of the family tree, 'Abd al-Radi is related to the mentally abnormal uncle Bakhit, and this is balanced on his mother's side by the mentally abnormal uncle 'Abdallah. 'Abdallah's father, Mahmud, the grandfather of 'Abd al-Radi, was already eccentric. If anyone insulted him, he took it peacefully and did not resort to any curse words. 'Abdallah was even more eccentric: He appeared as the realization of his father. He was called 'Abdallah *al-itwal*, 'Abdallah the crazy. He worked as a fellah in Kiman, insofar as he worked at anything. He was brown-skinned and of rather hefty build. He had strikingly large eyes. He was very silent. When someone insulted him in anger, for instance with the commonly used *"yin 'al-abuk,"* "(May God) curse your father," he would take it quietly and not answer directly, as anyone else would. When his father Mahmud died, and the funeral procession with the corpse had reached the cemetery, 'Abdallah, in contrast to everyone else, was very pleased, and told the people, *"Kulu kulu—eshshele shelti wu-l-hamm hammi"* (Eat, eat, what is there is there. The caring is my responsibility). In other words, "He is dead now, but don't worry about the future. I'll take care of that." These words were not invented by 'Abdallah. Earlier an upright close relative had used these words at the burial of a family head. But when crazy 'Abdallah used them, they made an impression on people. 'Abdallah died a long time ago, perhaps a generation or so, from an illness. His ghost descended many times to mediums, for instance, on two women in the Qift area, who in the meantime have died. Recently he also appears occasionally through 'Abd al-Radi. Relatives built him a shrine in Kiman. The mother of 'Abd al-Radi, Khadija, no longer lives with her husband Hamed in Naj' al-Hijayri, but instead came back here; she is the servant *(naqiba)* in her brother's shrine. In the shrine stands the wooden honor chest of the shaykh, covered with a beautiful cloth; across the room stretches a cord from which hang all kinds of votive offerings—doum palm fruits, a colorful cloth, a shaykh's banner. The blind mother of 'Abd al-Radi, the *naqiba*, takes care of the cleanliness of the shrine, of the mats and the lighting; she also keeps the key. She gets a small present from visitors, especially from those who have made a vow to the shaykh, and is entitled to a share of the sacrificial offerings.

'Abd al-Radi's Life History before the Big Illness

In 1933 'Abd al-Radi was about thirty-two or thirty-three years old. He spent his childhood and youth in Naj' al-Hijayri. Life flowed on in play, and then in peasant work like that of any fellah lad, without any noteworthy event. When he was about twenty years old he married Fatma, from the Shawadi family. This family is friendly with the maternal family of 'Abd al-Radi, the Atwal. Fatma has been 'Abd al-Radi's only wife until now. The relationship between the married couple has always been good, and remains so. This is even perceptible to the outsider who glimpses into the household life. Fatma bore him in total four children. The two eldest died when they were around two years old. The other two are still alive—a boy of four or five, and a girl of about three—as of the end of 1933 (see Plate 1).

'Abd al-Radi never learned to read and write. He was not very concerned with religious problems. He was a good Muslim, like other fellahin. He had never been more than just a spectator at the devotional exercises of the *zikr*. He had never visited a shaykh to whom a ghost had descended. On the contrary, when it came to that he was an outspoken skeptic. He always said, "*Ma fish mashayikh*" (There are no shaykhs—in the sense of possessing ghosts). This skepticism did not represent a distinctive position, for many men and some individual women maintain that ghosts cannot descend.

After ʿAbd al-Radi had been working as a fellah in Najʿ al-Hijayri, he took up the opportunity, like many of his fellow villagers, to earn the attractive monthly salary of three pounds by taking up a job as a construction worker in Ismaʿiliya on the Suez Canal. In about the last seven years, before his illness, ʿAbd al-Radi went for months to Ismaʿiliya and engaged in heavy construction work. The stays lasted from four to nine months. Just before the outbreak of the illness ʿAbd al-Radi spent the longest period, nine months, away. Toward the end of this work period in Ismaʿiliya, the disease had already begun. It began there with fever and trembling.

I asked ʿAbd al-Radi if earlier in the case of injuries, stomachache, headache, or coughing, and similar he had ever feared that this might be a serious illness leading even to death. He denied this emphatically. If he had anything of the sort, he did not take it particularly seriously.

I also asked him if he had ever anticipated or had a foreboding of events, either waking or in a dream. He also denied this.

From the Big Illness to the Call

The illness of 'Abd al-Radi can be broken down into two parts. 'Abd al-Radi feels these are two separate illnesses. He means that the illness that began in Isma'iliya is the consequence of hard work, and a chill that came on top of that. One has to take into account that this rather frail man had been working for nine months in Isma'iliya. He returned home sick, with fever and fits of the shivers, then aches, especially in the head, later on in the lower end of the anterior thorax and in the legs. When he had headaches, 'Abd al-Radi felt the pain of the rapidly beating pulse in his skull. He did not cough. Most of all he had frequent serious attacks of vomiting. 'Abd al-Radi traced his loss of weight back to this vomiting. At night he had heavy episodes of sweating, so that you could wring out his shirt. This illness lasted seven months, with the first three the most serious. 'Abd al-Radi felt that this sickness was natural.

After that, 'Abd al-Radi felt himself healthy again, and for two months he returned to farming. Of course he was much weakened so that he could handle only light work, for instance sieving grain on the threshing ground.

After these two months, 'Abd al-Radi fell sick again. He felt that this sickness was not natural, but was 'from God,' 'from the shaykh.' He had no fever and did not vomit. His whole body was paralyzed, and he could grip nothing with his hand. He felt severe pains everywhere, but especially in the right side of the body. "The Lord God took me. The Lord God seizes from the right and the devil from the left." This illness lasted three months. The whole time 'Abd al-Radi was sitting, with his knees pulled up, on the same spot, his head hanging to the right side. His eyes were shut. He saw and heard nothing of what was going on around him. His good wife Fatma looked after him, poured water and milk into his mouth, and helped him with the pot when he had a need. Despite eating very little, "the stomach was full, because of God." During this illness, the limbs on his right side wasted down to the bones. Even at least half a year after this illness I found the right leg noticeably thinner, and the musculature weaker than on the left side.

1: 'Abd al-Radi with his children. On the right, the low entrance of the house.

2: 'Abd al-Radi in possession. In his left hand he holds the cap of a child, which one of the women has given to him as a *riha*.

3: 'Abd al-Radi in possession.

Left:
4: 'Abd al-Radi in possession. He is describing a trip, stretching his hand in front of him on the map and saying *pff pff*.

Below left:
5: 'Abd al-Radi in possession. This laugh is not the ugly, raucous laugh that could sometimes be observed.

Below right:
6: 'Abd al-Radi in possession. His breathing is as in a *zikr*.

7: 'Abd al-Radi wakes up from possession. He has suddenly collapsed, banging his back and head against the wall behind him and slowly opening his eyes.

8: The cupola of the shrine of Bakhit, connected on the right to 'Abd al-Radi's house, whose low entrance is barely visible. In front of the shrine is a straw fence to protect the sycamore seedling, and in front of that, at the foot of the wall, the trough. Standing is Hamed, 'Abd al-Radi's father, with two of his sons.

9: The front wall of Bakhit's shrine. See page 133.

10: The interior of Bakhit's shrine. Offerings are hung on the rope. See pages 35–36.

11: The door of the shrine between Naj' al-Hijayri and Kiman. The picture of the flag carrier perhaps influenced 'Abd al-Radi's call dream. See page 156.

The Call and the Irregular
Possessions in the First Period

After three months the illness lightened somewhat and 'Abd al-Radi was able to move a little and circulate. Perhaps at this time, he occasionally participated in *zikr*s, in which through gentle swaying of the body he could recite for himself the names of God, *Allah* or *allaha*, or the breathing *hh-h*, which has the same meaning. The relatives of 'Abd al-Radi report this, and also 'Abd al-Radi has an unsure, cloudy, perhaps not original memory of this. It is also possible that it was merely the wheezing or panting of an 'Abd al-Radi whose spirit was absent while he was squatting there that was understood by his relatives as a *zikr* performance.

One midday 'Abd al-Radi was sleeping on the clay bench in the shady entrance to the farmhouse. His father was sitting next to him. When 'Abd al-Radi awoke, he felt that precisely on his right side—and here in telling this 'Abd al-Radi indicated the middle of his forehead—and then out his right arm and right leg water poured, *trrrr*. 'Abd al-Radi grasped that this came from God. You could see water on the ground afterward, like the water that is left after you wash yourself. 'Abd al-Radi indicated a puddle the size of his hand. His father asked him, "What is this water?" 'Abd al-Radi responded, "Do I know?" Thereupon the 'shaykh' seized him very suddenly; in other words, from this moment on 'Abd al-Radi knew nothing more. He wandered in the hilly desert until sunset.

But he returned still in this state of seizure, entered the courtyard of his house, and threw himself on his knees, "since the shaykh said *yekhkh*," added 'Abd al-Radi to his report. *Yekhkh* is the call that a camel driver uses to order the camel to kneel. Later 'Abd al-Radi lay down to sleep, although he had not yet really returned to his regular consciousness.

In this night, 'Abd al-Radi had a dream which gave a completely new direction to his future life. He saw a figure in a white shirt and white trousers, with a green headdress, with a broad cheerful face, large eyes, and a full black beard, about a hand length long and projecting forward. This figure held a green pole to which was attached a white flag. The spirit said, "*khud*" (take). And 'Abd al-Radi took the flag from his hand. The figure spoke, "I am your uncle Bakhit, and you are my *ga'ud*, my young male camel. I love you." Then the figure sat on his shoulders.

In this way 'Abd al-Radi was chosen by the ghost Bakhit and called. Two days after this night vision, on a Friday, the shaykh descended on him.

This dream brought the long painful illness to an end. What the illness had prepared had now clearly broken through the consciousness of 'Abd al-Radi: In the future, he would no longer be the usual 'Abd al-Radi, but would know that a ghost was making use of him and would ride him, that in the future he would have to support this ghost.

'Abd al-Radi told me that the ghost had never spoken to him again, although he frequently sees him in dreams. The call came to him a good half a year before I began my research in December 1933. The fellah has no record of events in historical order, and 'Abd al-Radi, who plays host to two or more personalities, certainly has no historical sense. The call-dream is protected in its contents by the incredibly solid, strong impression that it left in 'Abd al-Radi. But subsequently many other expressions of Bakhit have attached themselves to this event, some of which must have come from later dreams. An even greater part comes from the expressions of the possessing spirit—these wishes and communications that come from "Bakhit" must be explained to 'Abd al-Radi by his relatives after he awakes from the possession, "after the departure of Bakhit." And 'Abd al-Radi then links these for him very meaningful expressions to Bakhit's intrusion into his soul, to the call-dream. So today many of Bakhit's prescriptions are organized around the call-dream, so that it seems improbable that a single dream could have contained so much. I stress however that the core of the call-dream as against these later additions appears clearly delimited. Let us now look at what has gradually been collected around the call-dream.

In the accounts presented above on the saints and the dead in the Qift area, we saw many times that a ghost appeared through a medium to demand from his relatives a grave monument or a sanctuary for himself. That was also the first thing Bakhit demanded when he manifested himself through 'Abd al-Radi. After 'Abd al-Radi awoke this demand was naturally discussed in the family. 'Abd al-Radi—who never remembered what Bakhit said through him while he was possessed—heard of this demand (request), and in memory this request of Bakhit expressed during the possession flowed together with the call-dream. So we can recognize the first secondary addition to Bakhit's wishes—that a shrine in his honor should be built next to the house, that a sycamore seedling should be planted in front of the shrine, so that the sycamore would later shade the shrine and with this shade would also refresh the passersby, and finally that in front of the sycamore, directly on the street, a watering trough and a public fountain (sabil) should be established.

Soon the thought of what would happen to 'Abd al-Radi and his children must have worried him, since it was obvious that he no longer had the full strength of a fellah, and by following the life of a ghost-mount would never recover this strength. And again the consolation that he found in some depths of his soul connected with the call-dream: Shaykh Bakhit told him concerning his worried question about the future, "*Ana addilak min rizg 'and Allah*" (I will give you enough for your household, from God's grace).

'Abd al-Radi discovered that in spite of the gradually returning strength he was unable to perform with his wife any more. Here too Shaykh Bakhit intervened and explained. And this announcement was also incorporated into the call-dream. "The descent of the shaykh to you is a blessing, *baraka*, from God. Whoever is selected for this blessing must renounce the pleasure of a wife and children."

Very quickly the descents of the shaykh acquired their own regularity. He appeared precisely on given days and at given times. 'Abd al-Radi also understood that this regularity had been announced in the call-dream.

Possession was facilitated by the inhaling of incense, which also eased the transition to possession. Bakhit is also supposed to have said in the call-dream that the incense *jawli* (correctly *jawi*, benzoin) is especially agreeable to him.

Possession by a ghost is a religious event. It is understandable that the preparation, the dedication of 'Abd al-Radi on the days when he expects the descent of the ghost, begins a couple of hours before the possession with fasting, in other words, he avoids eating and drinking. Next to prayer, fasting is the principal religious act for Muslims, so it is certainly an obvious choice. Bakhit is also said to have ordered the fasting in the call-dream.

We know of the historical Bakhit that he liked to wander around in the desert hills. During possession Bakhit speaks through 'Abd al-Radi, occasionally giving a few mystic verses which relate to the desert and the saints. These verses probably originate in some *zikr* text. Bakhit is supposed to have pronounced them already in the call-dream. I heard these verses a couple of times from 'Abd al-Radi while he was possessed. Naturally, because of this repetition, they have also become well known to 'Abd al-Radi's relatives as a body of thought. Once when 'Abd al-Radi was visiting me and we were sitting in intimate conversation on a bench, I asked him again about these verses. 'Abd al-Radi said that Bakhit loved these verses because he loved being alone. Then he dictated them to me word by word, the way someone would communicate something confidential and very beautiful to a close friend. His voice was subdued and somewhat emotional. After I had written them down and read them back to him, he said, "That is something very lovely." Here are the verses:

. . . *al-gabal suwah*
. . . *al-handal wullihlah*
. . . *hili lihum*

guwa 'lmagam
rakhyin 'adabihum
barra ya khali barra
lasibik balawihum

yabu muntal
. . . mali minen
min mazayinhum
la salaba wa la muntal
al-gutb zayirhum

In the desert hills wandering alone
Colocynth and *lihlah*
Are sweet to them.

Inside shrines
Untied are their headscarves
Out you emptiness out,
Their disaster will meet you.

Oh man with the water-scoop
Full from where?
Of their jars
Not well-cord and not water-scoop
The *qutb* visits them.

These are verse fragments. They cannot be understood as a coherent text, but as images strung together, and furthermore meaningless images, expressionistic sketches. The verses validate, in 'Abd al-Radi's interpretation, the *mashayikh*, the ghosts. They are what wanders in the desert and make the bitter fruits of the desert appear sweet. This is also what is sung in the *zar* ceremonies, that the bitter fruits such as colocynth[5] are sweet to the *zar* spirits. *Magam* is explained as "saintliness, holy spot, where ghosts can be found." *Khali* (empty) is that person who does not belong to the shaykhs, and "whose headscarves thus hang down loosened." He is an intruder in holy places and will be chased away. "Man with the water-scoop"—the water-scoop is somehow a scoop of miracles or blessing. The jars, *zir* (pl. *muzayir*), are the large clay water jars, which in each peasant house keep the drinking water cool. Here

---

5 *Citrullus colocynthis*. NSH

the reference is to the jars of the shaykh. *Qutb* (pole) is the mysterious, cosmic carrier of divine knowledge in every era according to the teaching of Muslim mystics.

Taken together, these prescriptions, which laid out the new life pattern for 'Abd al-Radi, were doubtless not all combined in a single dream, but were given gradually in the early days of possession. Thus, 'Abd al-Radi unconsciously attached them all to the call-dream since they represent for him the final healing and the resulting strength.

We have once again to put ourselves in the present, the time immediately after the call, in order to see how gradually the new life pattern of 'Abd al-Radi came into being.

First of all, 'Abd al-Radi's relatives were not at all happy that 'Abd al-Radi was possessed by a shaykh. On the one hand, they were skeptical in general; on the other hand, the shaykh came with expensive demands. The first of Bakhit's demands was the construction of a shrine, the planting of the sycamore seedling, the installation of a public fountain. In order to pay for these demands Bakhit told Hamed, his brother, "Pay for the shroud." We can recall that the mayor of Kharishiya, at whose house Bakhit died, had provided the burial shroud, thus saving Hamed the expense. It is understandable that he didn't much like this reminder of a debt that had lapsed a generation ago. Nevertheless he brought out ten piasters, and handed them to 'Abd al-Radi, who then embodied Bakhit. Thereupon the shaykh got angry: "What? Ten piasters? Add another *riyal* (twenty piasters)." Hamed grumbled that he did not have a *riyal*. Then the painful miracle occurred. Hamed became mute. Only later, when he brought the *riyal*, did he recover his speech. With this money in hand, the construction of the shrine could begin.

Soon after the news spread that a new shaykh had appeared in Naj' al-Hijayri, people came to seek his advice. As is the practice, they brought a *riha*, a smell or token, from the one on whose behalf they wanted information, and with the *riha* a money gift. Now the father, Hamed, wanted to take the money from his son after he woke up from possession, for, he said "Bakhit is after all my brother." "Then Bakhit got angry" and didn't want to descend any more. 'Abd al-Radi was content with this. A good many days passed, and the shaykh did not appear. 'Abd al-Radi began to work in the fields a little. Then a week later as he was in the fields with his hoe, the shaykh suddenly took him. 'Abd al-Radi fell into possession and hit himself terribly with his hands, in the face, on the body, on the legs. "The shaykh hit me," said 'Abd al-Radi. Still in possession he ran home and sat in the usual spot in his yard. Since then he has stayed home and the shaykh descends regularly.

Now people looked favorably on 'Abd al-Radi's possession. But they still doubted that the ghost of Bakhit was the cause. They thought it might be something from underground, a *jinn*, or even *shaytan*, which had entered into him and taken on the mask of Bakhit. So the relatives invited a scholar to come. He pinched 'Abd al-Radi on the ear lobe during a possession and recited passages from the Qur'an, including the throne verse, into his ear and threatened to drive the spirit out. But thereupon Bakhit spoke through 'Abd al-Radi, "I am not one of the *jinn*. I am Bakhit. 'Abd al-Radi should be happy, and you should all be happy as this is a blessing." Then the shaykh legitimated himself even more by recounting how during his lifetime under such and such circumstances he had stolen pomegranates from his uncle's garden and given them away, and how he had been beaten for it. And he reminded Hamed how he had once beaten him because he ate so much, and how he, Bakhit, had gone away crying. Thus the simple-minded Bakhit stood clearly before the memory of all the old people, and they were persuaded that he was now really present in 'Abd al-Radi. This conviction was strengthened because the ghost kept returning, and did not kill 'Abd al-Radi, which is what a demon would have done.

Regular Possession Episodes

Time and Place

Shaykh Bakhit appears in 'Abd al-Radi on Monday until the afternoon prayer, on Wednesday after the afternoon prayer, all day on Thursday, and on Friday until the noon prayer. At these times, 'Abd al-Radi withdraws to the *khilwa*, the yard in his house, which is considered "holy," where mats are laid out and which is shaded by a thatched roof. The clients also come in here. They are segregated by sex. Usually the women come to him first; when they are done, then the men can enter. In the larger space in front of the *khilwa* yard the visitors can wait; they find shaded clay benches and a rope stretched above the ground where donkeys can be tied. 'Abd al-Radi goes regularly to his *khilwa* at the time of the expected descent of the shaykh. He is convinced the shaykh comes at the appointed time under any circumstances, irrespective of the place. But he also worries that the shaykh may become "angry" and appear in a foul mood if he cannot find him, 'Abd al-Radi, at the usual place. The appearance of the shaykh is also independent of whether clients are present or not. However, the possessions do not last long when there are no questions for the shaykh.

Beginning and Ending of Possession
Yawning
On the days when the shaykh descends, 'Abd al-Radi always yawns an unusual amount, beginning at least two hours before entering into possession. He also yawns in the short breaks between two possession episodes. Once, since the possession episode was slow in coming, I counted that 'Abd al-Radi yawned about thirty times in a quarter of an hour. I had the impression that 'Abd al-Radi could not yawn enough to satisfy himself.

Incense Burning and the Onset of Possession
Burning incense is universally appreciated in Egypt as a way to improve mood. In city alleys and bars one often enough sees poor devils swinging an incense pot, hoping to earn a small tip for this refreshment. Incense is also used to cure illnesses of man and beast, and is used in the mosques, but frankly I do not know to what extent and on which occasions this is customary in the rural areas around Qift. That 'Abd al-Radi also uses incense is thus nothing special. But the effect of incense on 'Abd al-Radi strikes me as essential.

The incense pot that 'Abd al-Radi uses is a spherical clay jug with a handle (see illustration). The lower half serves to hold the embers

while the upper half is not closed but rather features three ribs that serve as handles for the jug. These three ribs come together to form a tiny little dish on top. In this little dish lie ready the seeds of the incense. 'Abd al-Radi uses *jawli*—"its smell is very lovely." We know that in 'Abd al-Radi's thinking Shaykh Bakhit recommended this scent. One can take a couple of seeds from the little dish and toss them on the embers, and then immediately thin fumes arise.

'Abd al-Radi said, "Shaykh Bakhit loves incense. If he comes and finds no incense, he gets angry and hits me"; in other words, the possession begins very violently and 'Abd al-Radi's body is jolted and shaken. This is why

'Abd al-Radi uses incense to begin each first possession on a day when he expects the shaykh. If 'Abd al-Radi wakes out of possession after ten minutes, a quarter or half an hour, or a whole hour—the times vary greatly—then sometimes the second or third possession episode is induced through renewed censing, but these later possession episodes often come even without this preparation. Also, when 'Abd al-Radi wishes to induce a possession outside the scheduled times, the incense helps him do that—not necessarily, but as a rule.

I mentioned above how 'Abd al-Radi once had difficulty entering into a state of possession, and how in the long drawn-out wait he yawned again and again. 'Abd al-Radi had his younger brother, about eighteen years old, who often took care of these matters, rekindling the embers in the pot and throwing a couple of incense seeds into them. 'Abd al-Radi squatted in his place, only half aware. As soon as the smell reached his nose, possession came suddenly and sharply. He quickly fell to his knees, picked up the pot, brought it very close to his face, and drank in the fumes through mouth and nose with openly sensuous desire. Bakhit could often be observed eagerly inhaling the smoke. More often than not, the first scent was enough to bring about the appearance of the ghost, and the customary deep drinking didn't happen. For example, once 'Abd al-Radi sat waiting for the commencement of possession. His facial expression was visibly more and more tired. He rocked his torso very lightly from one side to the other. When therefore a breath of incense met his face, he began to tremble slightly. Possession had been achieved.

Shortness of Breath

This inhaling of fumes and its effect on 'Abd al-Radi directs our attention to the meaning of breath and breathing for the state of possession. We can recall the yawning prior to possession. I often had the impression that, at the onset of possession, 'Abd al-Radi seemed about to be flooded by a wave—he breathed rapidly and convulsively, as if about to drown. The words that he was to utter first—brief, soft, with light breath, sounded very much like a call for help by someone sinking into water. After this "flooding," this intrusion of the shaykh, he then recovered his breath and his voice gradually became firm and strong.

The Ending

The appearance of Bakhit and the other ghosts who showed themselves in the possessed will soon be characterized. But first we have to describe how the possession episode ends. The end is as remarkable as the beginning (see Plate 7).

During the possession, one had throughout the impression that another personality, such as Bakhit, or other personalities, other spirits or ghosts, appeared in 'Abd al-Radi and spoke. Of course the pantomime and the vocal changes remained in the realm of 'Abd al-Radi's natural possibilities. But each ghost had his clearly indicated individual traits, which equally distinguished him from the other ghosts or, naturally, from 'Abd al-Radi himself. Just as the possession began without mediation, so also it broke off in that way. Often completely unexpected, in the midst of an announcement, the taut face of 'Abd al-Radi collapsed. The torso, usually held upright on the knees, fell back onto the heels, the back crumpled and hit against the wall in front of which 'Abd al-Radi sits, and even the head knocked gently against this wall. It appeared as if a body that had been held upright by another hand was suddenly released, as if the body had fallen from above, a body that no longer had a will and was as relaxed as that of a sleeping person. 'Abd al-Radi's eyes, during possession, were either tightly closed, or the lids fell over the pupils; rarely were the eyes wide open, and so the gaze was veiled. Now after waking up from possession, 'Abd al-Radi opened his eyes slowly and, as if tired, the gaze returned to its natural sharpness, the facial expression showed suffering, the voice shy and weak. Still only half awake, as a rule 'Abd al-Radi recited to the gathering the profession of the faith: "I testify that there is no God but God and that Muhammad is his Prophet." 'Abd al-Radi then looked around at those sitting with him, and often greeted them, apparently surprised to find himself with guests.

The role of the breath is also distinctive here. I often observed how 'Abd al-Radi toward the end of a lengthy possession episode pulled nervously on the point and wings of his nose, and stuck his fingers a little in the nostrils, and once beat himself on the nose. The meaning of this gesture became clear when he once gently pressed on the wings of his nose and said, "*Ruh*" (leave). So it seems that 'Abd al-Radi inhales the spirit with his breath, and then exhales him again with the breath.

We will return later to the question of whether in this last-mentioned example, while still possessed by Bakhit, 'Abd al-Radi himself, out of the depths of his soul, rose up and tried to shake off the spirit.

The Spirits of Possession
Bakhit

We know that when Bakhit was alive he was a simpleton, was unable to do any work, but was a carrier of mysterious blessings, both dangerous and fortunate. A generation after his death he fixed his love on 'Abd al-Radi and chose him as his mount, and transformed this fellah into a door between the human world and the spirits of the dead. Bakhit is the master of 'Abd al-Radi, but the spirits of other departed souls also at times pass through this door in connection with the living. Each ghost has particular features by which he can be recognized.

Bakhit told 'Abd al-Radi in the call-dream, "You will be my he-camel." The handler says "*yekh*" to the camel when the beast is supposed to drop down to its knees. Then the camel bends his knees, slowly at first, and with tense muscles, until the weight of the bending body becomes stronger than the elasticity of the muscles, which are holding the leg in a bent position. Then the beast falls on its calloused knees and lies upright, now on the knees and stomach. This obedient, deliberate, awkward kneeling of the powerful beast leaves an impression. When Shaykh Bakhit takes him over, one can see that 'Abd al-Radi really is his *ga'ud*, his male camel. One sees how 'Abd al-Radi squats in his place, and prepares to take on the possession. His face is somewhat passive and absent, one feels that his consciousness is sinking away, then suddenly he raises himself out of the squatting position and pushes hard with the knees against the earth; the he-camel has lowered himself to his knees and the rider is there. Rising up to a kneeling position is the characteristic gesture signaling the appearance of Bakhit.

I reported that the entry of Bakhit causes 'Abd al-Radi to catch his breath and his breath simultaneously bursts out, so that then the possession breaks over 'Abd al-Radi like a wave. Most often 'Abd al-Radi begins then to breathe in and out as if the muscles of the mouth were paralyzed. The tongue then jumps around in the flow of inhaled breath vibrating in the mouth and produces a gurgling sound, and the exhaling breath blows past the slack lips of an almost closed mouth. The lips are vibrating as when we imitate a snorting horse. The he-camel can emit a special gurgling sound from his chest, while a throaty foam is pushed forward in the front of the mouth. It is not improbable that the gurgling and snorting of 'Abd al-Radi at the beginning of his possession by Bakhit is a representation of the kneeling camel. We can also recall that Bakhit in his lifetime is said to have articulated distinctive lip sounds, *pupu pupu*.

Quite often in the possession by Bakhit we can observe elements from the *zikr*, usually directly following the gurgling and snorting, sometimes in the middle of his message. 'Abd al-Radi then rises upright on his knees, swaying his body slowly from side to side or from front to back, with his head tilted back and a solemn facial expression. He breathes in short breaths, he breathes in two or three times while deep in the back of his mouth he articulates *h-h-h*, then exhales in a long stroke, *hh*, and then continues in rapid repetition (see Plate 6).

Bakhit uses religious expressions at the beginning of his possession with great regularity. Just as 'Abd al-Radi, when pulling himself together or awakening from possession, repeats first of all the profession of faith, so Bakhit uses these expressions to present himself and to legitimate himself as a right-believing ghost. Often the voice at the beginning of the possession, while still under the influence of the disappearing shortness of breath, is low and soft. The words pour out in a rush. Often he says, "All Muslims bless the Prophet." Sometimes he asks the visitors to repeat with him the profession of faith. The order to bless the Prophet is often given by Bakhit in the middle of his "prophecy." Bakhit also calls for the *Fatiha*, the opening *sura* of the Qur'an, from time to time, without any special impetus from the clients, and naturally he joins in.

These religious expressions remind us of the mystical verses of the saints who wander in the desert, which Bakhit presumably referred to in the call-dream, and which in the circumstances of possession from time to time were referred to by the ghost, as special high points of the solemn mood, and which were applauded by the guests with wonder.

However, the ghost Bakhit is on the whole not solemn, but instead is blustering, rude, and sometimes a bit childish. He laughs easily—sometimes this laugh is so obscene and shameless that it seems vulgar.

We know that the historic Bakhit did not speak much and that when he spoke he loved all kinds of speech novelties. The speech of Bakhit the ghost also has its peculiarities. To begin with, the full prophecy never comes forth as complete utterances, but is brief, often obscure, often however in unambiguously striking sentences that relate to the client's case. Even here, however, the individual words often undergo sound shifts. This resembles what happens when an adult tries to imitate the speech of a two- or three-year-old child. This may be attributed to the image of a simple-minded Bakhit, or it could follow from the sometimes partly paralyzed mouth muscles, which simplify the difficult sounds and clusters. The lips are then often extruded as in an animal's snout.

These transformations of individual words do not always occur but they usually do. One can observe the following patterns:

Voiced sounds become voiceless. I heard, for instance:
tabih for *dabih* (sacrifice)
atyan for *adyan* (religions)
kite for *kide* (thus)
bis(i)yata for *biziyada* (very)
awlat for *awlad* (children)
mosh (the sibilant not very clear but more *mosh* than *mos*) for
    muz (banana plant)

The sound of *r* becomes *l*, for instance:
las for *ras* (head)
luh for *ruh* (go away)
ya labbi for *ya rabbi* (O God)
alba'a wu'alba'in for *arba'a wu'arba'in* (forty-four)
'alif for *'arif* (knowing)
balla for *barra* (outside)
belsim for *bersim* (clover)
malhaba for *marhaba* (welcome)
ishlab for *ishrab* (drink)

S becomes *sh*, for instance:
shalat for *salat* (prayer)
yishalli for *yisalli* (he prays)
bashal for *basal* (onion)
khalash for *khalas* (ready, done)

J is simplified in several ways, for instance:

tyamusa for *jamusa* (water buffalo)

tyabal for *jabal* (mountain)

dyawab and *dawab* for *jawab* (letter)

doza for *joza* (water pipe)

mawdud for *mawjud* (present)

rikal for *rijal* (men)

Consonant clusters are assimilated, separated by a vowel, or
   one of the consonants is omitted, for instance:

itte for *inte* (you)

mattub for *maktub* (written)

abbahi for *idbahi* (bring a sacrifice)

idenayn and *denayn* for *itnayn* (two)

baten for *ba'dayn* (later)

senne shwoiya for *(i)stanne shwoiya* (wait a little)

dilbati for *dilwaqti* (now)

Among other occasional specificities, I observed:

karb and *kharb* for *gharb* (western)

ma bish for *ma fish* (there aren't any)

hu'um(a) for *hukuma* (government)

af(a)tan (exclamation) for *abadan* (never)

Words which the shaykh particularly liked would be playfully expanded
and repeated, e.g., *Aswan swan siwan*, or *ya Muhammad, ya Hammad, ya
Mahmud, ya Hamid (ya Hasan, ya Husayn), ya Muhammad.*

Unclear speech and the brief obscure sentences are completed by
onomatopoeia or gestures.

As examples of onomatopoeia I noted *pff pff pff* (railroad, trip), *tu
tu tu* (airplane or airmail letter). The bellowing of cattle was very ably
repeated, and distinctions were made between the squeaky sound of
the buffalo cow and the musical sound of the cow and the lighter one
of the calf. The cooing of the pigeon was represented somewhat imper-
fectly as *kukukuku*, the laughter of children as *krrr krrr*. Distinctive and
striking was the vocal symbolizing of the loneliness of the ravines in

the granite desert mountains with a dull hollow *hoo hooo*. The falling of a boulder would be sounded out by a long dying *drmmm*.

As for gestures I noticed the following: holding a hand horizontally close to the ground signified a small child. Raising and lowering a horizontal hand in the air meant children playing ball. Sometimes the gestures would be continued by clapping the hands, and moving both hands as if to catch the ball.

Using one hand to make a circular gesture horizontally on the floor mat or with both hands perpendicularly in the air—this was a frequent gesture, but I was unable to place a particular interpretation on it. I think it was a gesture of circumstance to fill out an empty pause in the prophecy.

To spit on the fist and then to move the fist as if to hit represented a blow or a boxing of the ears.

Kissing the hand signified proof of love of a distant relative. Frequently the kissing of the hand was directed to God, especially after saying the *Fatiha*.

Snapping the index or middle finger on the thumb signified a blow. This gesture is widely used here, as is the next one.

Rubbing the thumb on the index and middle fingers meant to pay out money. We have the same gesture.

Holding both hands in front of the face to represent a book meant reading.

Drawing the right index finger over the inner side of the flat left hand meant writing. Notably, this gesture of writing would regularly go from left to right, although writing in Arabic runs from right to left. We recall that 'Abd al-Radi is illiterate.

Holding the two hands together next to the mouth with moving fingers meant playing the flute.

Drawing the index finger of one hand back and forth between the index and middle fingers of the other one. This unmistakable gesture means kinship through the marriage bed, in-law relations. Shaykh Bakhit took pleasure in this indecent gesture and would continue making it until the embarrassed client would say, "*fihimt*" (I understand, I get it).

Laying the right hand on the cheek, tilting the head to the right, eyes closed meant sleeping, also thinking.

Laying the hand on the chin and brushing it forward signified a bearded man, an elder. The gesture was also used when the old man referred to did not have a beard at all.

Rapid hand movements toward the heart indicated illness and pain.

Passing the hand over the robe meant beautiful clothes, air of distinction.

Putting the index finger in the mouth and sucking on it signified a water pipe (*goza*) smoker.

These gestures bring us to the essential performance of the ghost of Bakhit: He is clairvoyant, a seer. We will see more of this in the rest of the text. When Bakhit, speaking through 'Abd al-Radi, refers to a letter that is on the way or announces the imminent arrival of someone, or when he describes a distant house and the people in it, then 'Abd al-Radi often raises his hand in the direction of this letter, person, or house, he looks there with glassy eyes, and says "*aho aho*" (look there, look there, I see it). 'Abd al-Radi in possession seems really to see these distant things. Facial expressions make it possible for him to display this knowledge of the faraway and the hidden.

Other Spirits

Bakhit is the uncontested master of 'Abd al-Radi. He chose him and he descends on him regularly. But once that happens, once *one* ghost, in this case Bakhit, breaks through to the human world through 'Abd al-Radi—a passageway between the world of the dead and of the living is opened up. Thus it is not at all surprising that other departed souls can also enter through this passageway. In speaking of the spirits of the dead we place ourselves completely in the position of our Upper Egyptian peasants, in order to enumerate the images of the individual ghosts as clearly as possible. 'Abd al-Radi, who at least from his conversations with his guests and relatives hears what kind of ghosts had entered into him while he was possessed, thinks of all these ghosts as friends of Bakhit, as a "team" that he heads in another world.

Shaykh 'Ali

In Naj' al-Hijayri people respect Shaykh 'Ali, who died two generations ago (see p. 45). His sanctuary is on the edge of the village. He often comes down through 'Abd al-Radi. Bakhit can be recognized because the medium usually kneels; 'Ali is known because he clenches his arms tightly across his chest. In Naj' al-Hijayri lives a well-to-do man, Mahmud, whose wife had not borne children. Shaykh 'Ali appeared to this man at night in a nightmare, crouched on his chest, so that he felt anxiety and fear. He then went to 'Abd al-Radi to seek advice and a cure. When 'Abd al-Radi fell into possession, Bakhit did not appear, but instead Shaykh 'Ali with folded arms. He told the man, "I want a bull-calf from you." Mahmud answered, "Why do you oppress me and why do you want a bull-calf? If you help my wife bear children, you can have the calf." Shaykh 'Ali said, "Bringing children is a matter for God but I want the calf." Mahmud promised the calf when his wife became pregnant. She actually then did become pregnant. When I first heard this story, she was already in the seventh month. The bull-calf was already in the stable. When the child was born the calf would be offered as a sacrifice at Shaykh 'Ali's shrine.

Shaykh 'Ali appears in particular to people from his family whom he advises through the medium 'Abd al-Radi about illnesses and other problems. He distinguishes himself from Bakhit by the gesture of the folded arms and also a solemn manner and gentle speech. Although he asks for sacrifices for his own shrine, he does not forget the medium. "Bring this and that as a present for the *ga'ud*," in other words, 'Abd al-Radi. I recall one session where Shaykh 'Ali was advising a great-nephew how he could recover from an illness. The great-nephew had already been there once and Shaykh 'Ali had asked for a scarf for the "he-camel." Shaykh 'Ali's ghost now asked, "Where is the scarf?" Then the young man with a triumphant if awkward smile pulled the gift from his robe. When Shaykh 'Ali departs from 'Abd al-Radi, he manages to shake and push him.

Muhammad Ahmad Yusuf al-Asyuti
Al-Asyuti is another spirit of the dead. He appears not infrequently. For this reason he is especially noteworthy, since no one in this place knew al-Asyuti when he was alive, and also he asks for nothing and gives no advice. When he appeared for the first time, the relatives and guests of 'Abd al-Radi noticed that he was a foreign ghost. He raised his right hand, and then began to sway the kneeling, upright body lightly and slowly, and to sing with a beautiful full voice, "*Ya da'im, ya da'im,*

ya daim," ("O eternal, O eternal, O eternal"). The people were puzzled and asked, "Who are you?" He answered, half singing and half speaking, "I am Muhammad Ahmad Yusuf al-Asyuti." He always appears in this way, singing fervently and ecstatically, "O eternal, O eternal." And no one knows when and where he lived and died.

Muhammad 'Abd al-Qadir of Barahma

Muhammad 'Abd al-Qadir was a railroad employee when he was alive. He handled the signals at the Qift railroad station. He was married and had a baby daughter. One evening he went as usual to work from his village of Barahma. That night he fell under a train that ran over and killed him. This was probably an accident, but in the heart of the dead man's parents there remained a doubt that their son might have had enemies who pushed him under the train. One night the mother of the victim glimpsed her son in a dream. He told her, "Go to 'Abd al-Radi in Naj' al-Hijayri, you will find me there." So the parents went to 'Abd al-Radi. The ghost of their son appeared through the medium. One cannot think of the fellah as a blockhead unable to think critically. The fellah is supposed to bring a present for his consultation with the vehicle of the ghost. Even if it is only a millieme or a basket of dates, he does not give it at first in order not to be duped by a swindler. 'Abd al-Qadir, the father of the victim, resolved to test the ghost who called himself his son. I was lucky enough that by chance I was sitting next to 'Abd al-Radi when the father and the ghost of his son met each other for the second time. The father was a man of about sixty, with an unusually thick, broad nose, a fellah like the other guests. Around his neck there hung a dark blue ribbon with occasional red knots of wool; probably his purse hung from that. He had wrapped a bunch of dates in a cloth, and had that in his hand. He shoved this over to 'Abd al-Radi. Now I follow the description I jotted down in my diary immediately after the session.

The incense pot was brought. After the first delicate incense fumes reached him, 'Abd al-Radi rose from his squatting position upright onto his knees. Bakhit entered into him. He grasped the incense pot energetically, brought it up like a water pot to his face, and drank in the fumes. Then he lowered it, and swung it back and forth over the mat a couple of times. Then he squatted again on his heels. Head, torso, and hands were dancing equally in tandem. He breathed in several breaths, and with each breath came a suppressed short sound. After about a minute of such breathing he spoke with an abrupt, shy, yet clear voice, "All Muslims should bless the Prophet." Then he turned to a fellah sitting to his right, a man in his mid-thirties, with a sorrowful credulous face. This man passed to the shaykh a crumpled-up black thread of wool as a *riba*. The shaykh took and felt the wool thread in his hand, and soon found the right path. The obscure fragments of the information were only comprehensible to the concerned party. I see from his tense but attentive face: He understands the message of Bakhit and agrees. Gradually the speech becomes clearer. We also understand. The wife of the petitioner is sick, the sickness is in her body and is severe, she has pain in her knee. After the symptoms have been described, Bakhit prescribes the cure. It mostly involves lemons. She should take this for seven days.

Now the old man from Barahma edges closer to 'Abd al-Radi. He sits in the right corner near 'Abd al-Radi. 'Abd al-Radi rises to his knees. His face has now clearly changed. The expression is noble and solemn. There is deathly silence. The medium turns his upper body slowly halfway to the right, toward the old man from Barahma, and rubs himself slowly with the right hand across the middle of the body, as if to indicate cutting it in two. The chin is slightly raised, I see the profile. The lips are protruded outward. It all seems very beautiful, I might say, exalted or noble, this solemn face. In a barely audible whisper, the ghost speaks to the old man, "*Salam 'alaykum.*" Roughly and loudly and disturbed, Hamed, the father of 'Abd al-Radi, asks the ghost, "Who are you?" He answered again, in a very soft voice, "I am Muhammad 'Abd al-Qadir from Barahma." The old man from Barahma now asks this ghost, who claims to be his son, "What did we have to eat at home in the evening, the last time you went to work?" The ghost whispers, "We were supposed to eat a turkey-cock. But it was not yet cooked. I told my mother, cut off a piece for me for tomorrow morning. I am going to work and I am taking radishes." My mother said, "Bring a sugar cone and tea back from the town." The old man begins to cry, tears come from his eyes and flow down his wrinkled cheeks. There is no more doubt, his son's ghost is there. He asks, "My son, were you killed because of God's will, in an accident, or were you killed by enemies?" The ghost makes a gesture of denial—he moves his right hand slowly and gravely with a raised index finger back and forth, and whispers, "*Amru, amru*," (his command, his command). The old man takes up the word and says, "*Amru, amru*," and Hamed, 'Abd al-Radi's old father, also repeats this, *amru*. The ghost then whispers, "Father and mother should not cry so, he, the ghost, has sore cheeks because of these tears." Then he begins to grope for the old man's head. The father holds quite still. He runs his hand over the father's head. Stiffly he remains there. Then he leans slowly to the skull of the old man and kisses his headcloth. The old man's tears flow freely. He bends forward a second time and kisses his headcloth. A third and a fourth time. "Don't cry," he whispers.

Then the picture changed. 'Abd al-Radi fell back suddenly and banged against the wall behind him a couple of times, as if a foreign hand were pushing him there. This was now Shaykh 'Ali who was shaking him. The father of 'Abd al-Radi called out, loud and full of concern, "*Ga'udak*, your he-camel," in other words, "O Bakhit, this is for sure your faithful he-camel, why are you letting him be pushed around?" The pushing stopped, the body of 'Abd al-Radi was quickly again upright. He begins to sing, his right hand raised, "O eternal, O eternal, O eternal." The facial expression is now different: Al-Asyuti has appeared. After hardly a minute, 'Abd al-Radi again fell back, then quickly sat upright again: with a gurgling tongue and flabby lips Bakhit appeared. In the usual style he took a *riha* from a visitor, and with obscure gestures and words detailed for him a message, in the meantime laughing in his ugly and unpleasant way. Then he fell back unexpectedly. The possession came to an end. 'Abd al-Radi opened his tired eyes. "Praise God," said his relieved father. After a while, 'Abd al-Radi picked up the bundle that the old man from Barahma had brought as a present, and found a couple of pounds of dates. Quite tactfully, 'Abd al-Radi took the present which he had received on behalf of this strange ghost and divided it among the guests. Each one got a handful of dates. In the corner a couple of women were squatting—they were in a hurry, they wanted to be alone with the shaykh, and had a long road home.

The old man from Barahma came several more times to 'Abd al-Radi and each time the ghost of his dead son appeared to him. Two months later I was again present. That time Bakhit was the first to appear, then al-Asyuti, and then this Muhammad 'Abd al-Qadir. Once again he knelt upright and gravely, and once again he presented himself through the gestures of the passage, the rubbing of the chest. With a gentle, childlike voice he and the old man whispered together. Then he kissed the old man's hand, then his headcloth, then once more the hand. The old man wiped tears from his eyes. Hamed brought coffee for the guests, each one drank a cup, including 'Abd al-Qadir in the presence of the ghost of his dead son. After a while the ghost began to sing happily. Delivery, timbre, and words were unlike those of the singing of al-Asyuti; this was in praise of God; then 'Abd al-Radi fell back from his upright position, and with flabby lips the blustery Bakhit appeared. Then the old 'Abd al-Qadir asked Bakhit where his son—his dead son's ghost—had gone, since he had just been present. Bakhit said, "He is in Aswan, siwan, siwan"—he toyed with the word lovingly and dreamily. We will see later that Aswan is understood here as the homeland of the ghosts.

Muhammad Ahmad of al-Qal'a

I experienced the appearance of this ghost once, when a whole sequence of foreign ghosts revealed themselves in short order in 'Abd al-Radi. When this Muhammad Ahmad died as a boy in the nearby village of al-Qal'a, he refused to go to the cemetery. Rather, he obliged the pall-bearers of his coffin to return from the cemetery to his house. The mourners recited potent pious sayings. Then they set out again for the cemetery, and with better luck: The bearers could deposit and bury the dead body. Shortly afterward the father of this youth fell sick: "The shaykh—the ghost of his dead son—took hold of his feet and hands, and grabbed him on the head and back." The man set out with his wife to see 'Abd al-Radi, in order to ask Bakhit, or even to hear directly from their own son. It so happened that Bakhit had just been present in the medium in a blustery appearance, but then the behavior suddenly changed. 'Abd al-Radi made himself seem small, unwound his head-cloth, pulled his shaved skull down between his shoulders, bent his back, smiled continually, and turned to the old man from al-Qal'a, sitting to his right, then to his wife, sitting on his left. He was now the ghost of Muhammad, the dead son of these two. He kissed the old man's hand, then his wife's, kissed them warmly for a full moment, and the woman kissed his hand again. The old man observed him with a smile on his face but with doubt in his eyes. A cousin of the deceased Muhammad had come with the married couple. The ghost now also greeted him. The old man had come to seek advice for his illness. The ghost of his dead son explained to him, while continuing his childish smile, that he had caused this illness because he desired a memorial shrine surrounded by a wall near his parents' house. He (the ghost!) would show them the exact spot, by placing four bricks leaning on one another. While continuing to smile, he threatened to make the old man blind if he did not obey this order. The old man agreed, and all together recited the *Fatiha* to ratify this agreement. Then the ghost turned to the cousin—all the while smiling—and said, "If you get married soon, will you give the he-camel ['Abd al-Radi] a scarf?" The cousin said, "Yes." This was the situation with regard to the marriage: The lad wanted to marry a certain girl but had not yet been able to raise the bride price. He now wanted to give the girl's father an advance, and then pay the rest in installments. But the girl's father refused to entertain this plan. The ghost then said he would change the father's mind, but would need a vow. First of all, the cousin should distribute milk cakes to the poor at the village mosque; second, he should organize a *zikr*; and third, he should bring, after the marriage, a castrated ram as a sacrificial offering to his shrine. The cousin expressed agreement, and himself asked for the collective recitation of the *Fatiha* in order to sanctify the agreement.

'Ali from Barahma

In Barahma lived a man called 'Ali. He died and left behind two children, a boy and a girl. The mother then remarried. The two children stayed with their grandfather, the father of the deceased 'Ali. This grandfather was mean to the children. His eyes began to hurt, and he went to 'Abd al-Radi to find a prescription for them. When he arrived at 'Abd al-Radi's, he found that 'Abd al-Radi was possessed by Bakhit. Bakhit said to him, "You are responsible for the children of your dead son and you are mean to them." Then the ghost was transformed, and instead of Bakhit the ghost of the dead 'Ali appeared before his father. 'Ali began to cry. People saw that a different ghost had appeared and asked, "Who are you, why are you crying?" The ghost turned to the old man and spoke, "You are treating my son badly, he wanders around in the lanes, but you have also driven the girl out of the house. This is a shame, *'ar*, and is dangerous for the girl. You say that the girl is crazy *(majnuna)* and that a *zar* spirit is riding her. That is not true, she is not crazy and is not possessed by a *zar*. Give her the land I had chosen for her dowry, and of the cow that I left give half to the girl and half to the boy, then the girl will be able to marry. When you have done all this, collect from the fields some *harra* (*Coronopus niloticus* sp.), cook it, and let the vapor rise into your face; that will heal your eyes." The old man did as bidden.

Nur al-Din from 'Aqula

The village of 'Aqula lies about two hours south of Naj' al-Hijayri. A man called Nur al-Din died in this village. He left behind a young son. The father of Nur al-Din took responsibility for the child, but was not good to the child. He developed a bad ulcer on his leg. He came to 'Abd al-Radi to request a cure from the shaykh. Instead of Bakhit, the ghost of Nur al-Din came down. He reproached the father for his poor treatment of his son. The old man said stubbornly, "I am taking good care of him." The ghost answered, "I can see that you are not treating him well, and so I have made your leg sick." The old man promised to treat his grandson better. Then the ghost proposed a cure to him.

Khalifa Mustafa from al-Shaykhiya

He died some four years ago; now he appeared in 'Abd al-Radi when his mother was present and demanded that a walled memorial tomb be built for him. The ghost said that since his brothers had inherited from his father, they had enough money to carry out this wish. If his brothers should refuse to do this, he would send them illnesses or even death. These dark threats were accompanied by the ghost gently and solemnly kissing her hand. The mother returned this kiss on the hand, to be sure full of doubt and vexation.

Abbadi Muhammad Birudi

When living he was a boatman on the Nile. He fell into the river and drowned. Sometimes he appears in 'Abd al-Radi.

Wardani ibn al-Hajj al-Sughayar from Kiman

From childhood on Wardani was sickly, and died about 1931 in Kiman. From time to time he appears in 'Abd al-Radi. He is fond of sitting cross-legged and of repeating the *Fatiha* softly.

'Abd al-Qadir al-Jilani

This ghost seldom appears. Like al-Asyuti, he is fond of singing.

'Abdallah, 'Abd al-Radi's Uncle

He also descends very occasionally on 'Abd al-Radi.

Salim al-Huwi

Salim al-Huwi is considered a very well known shaykh (see pp. 45–46). Many people think that he is too important to come down on a medium, so they think that this might be another lesser ghost who appears in the guise of Huwi. He asks nothing of the living; he only appears, similar to an impressive adornment, when a large number of ghosts present themselves to 'Abd al-Radi's guests.

The brother of the simple-minded Shaykha Fatma, 'Abbas from Qift, who was suspected of being possessed, once consulted 'Abd al-Radi—we will return to this later. On that occasion there appeared in 'Abd al-Radi a whole series of ghosts one after the other, as if Bakhit on the far side had brought forward his whole team, so that perhaps one of them might help 'Abbas, or that through this procession of ghosts one would be attracted into appearing in him, or who might turn out to have seized 'Abbas. Bakhit appeared first in the well-known way, and shared a message with other people; then the situation changed. 'Abd al-Radi raised himself straight upward, pulled his shoulders forward, and folded his arms tightly—that was Shaykh 'Ali. He moved his lips inaudibly. "He is reciting from the Qur'an," said those sitting around. Shortly the manner changed again. 'Abd al-Radi threw his head back, raised his right hand, and began to sing "O eternal, O eternal" — this was al-Asyuti. Then the appearance changed again. 'Abd al-Radi sat cross-legged, recited the *Fatiha*, and identified himself as Wardani. Thus yet another new ghost appeared, happily singing, quite different from al-Asyuti's solemnity. "*Salam 'alaykum ya jalisin, salam 'alaykum, ana 'Abd al-Qadir al-Jilani*" ("Greetings to those sitting here, greetings. I am 'Abd al-Qadir al-Jilani"). This ghost also disappeared after a short visit, and the great Huwi honored us with his presence. He spoke softly in a squeaky low voice, all the while smiling. While he was speaking, he was continually driving away imaginary cats with gestures and by calling out "*bss bss aiya bss aiya bss bss.*" His shrine in Hu is said to be full of cats. He appeared to be funny and amused the visitors. In order to remove any doubt, he introduced himself, "I am Salim al-Huwi," and flattered himself by saying that no crocodile would pass his shrine on the Nile near Hu because he prevents this. After al-Huwi, Bakhit came again. Soon after came Muhammad Ahmad from al-Qal‘a with his childish smile, who had just threatened his father, who was present, with blindness, unless he built him a memorial tomb, as we recounted above.

After all these ghosts had passed through the medium, ‘Abd al-Radi woke out of his trance. The next one started immediately, and in this one Bakhit turned to the case of ‘Abbas.

A Double Possession

Only once did I experience the rare drama that, in addition to ‘Abd al-Radi, another person also fell into possession. This other was Musa, an elderly Abbadi with a brown, wrinkled face and a short white beard. The spirit who appeared in him is also an Abbadi, whose body is buried near Kom Ombo. The ‘Ababda are an African Bedouin people whose home is in the desert of Upper Egypt between the Nile and the Red Sea. Many ‘Ababda have settled on the edge of the Nile Valley in Upper Egypt and become farmers. This old man also belonged to the sedentarized ‘Ababda, though he is now drifting from place to place. I present this account of the meeting with the two possessed men directly from my diary. This occurred on December 24, 1933.

I went to Naj‘ al-Hijayri in the afternoon. ‘Abd al-Radi was completely possessed when I arrived. Shortly after I arrived an old man entered, completely or nearly blind, an Abbadi. He sat down to the right of ‘Abd al-Radi. A couple of fellahin were sitting there. To one of them Bakhit, mediated through ‘Abd al-Radi, was just then giving some information. ‘Abd al-Radi awoke from the possession, greeted me, and asked courteously what news I had of my wife and children. The incense pot was in front of him, its embers nearly extinguished. Suddenly ‘Abd al-Radi became possessed again. He shot straight up on his knees, making guttural noises with his tongue, and the lips trembled. He gave a message to one man, which had to do with something northward. The man objected; the shaykh insisted on his interpretation. Meanwhile he laughed in his unpleasant manner. Then he took my hand and advised me that my wife and children were healthy. A man, a friend, would come. I would travel away with him. In fifteen days.

'Abd al-Radi now turned to the right to the old Abbadi and took his hand. Suddenly with a lurch the old man was sitting in the middle of the mat, in the right corner to 'Abd al-Radi. He unwrapped his head-cloth. His white hair was rather long. As in a *zikr* be began to sway strongly, moving his torso backward and forward. The accuracy of the rhythm was extraordinary, as if it were timed by a metronome. The old man was sitting with his legs under him, his knees also beating hard and with increasing strength on the ground. The old man exhaled now as in the *zikr* in three-time, something like *allaha = h-h—hh*. Here too there was an extraordinary sureness of rhythm. The tongue from time to time made a distinctive gurgling sound. It was clearly visible how, when inhaling, the tongue is caught between the front teeth of the barely opened jaws, by the inhaling of air, and is then pushed back, and without tension immediately again falls forward and is grasped, then is pushed back, again falls forward, and so on in rapid succession. This is what produced the gurgling sound. Then he began to sing. The movement of the body became a rotation, from right forward to the left, that is counterclockwise. He was singing a legend about the gazelle who kissed the hand of the Prophet Muhammad, and about a Jew. The facial expression showed agony but also behind that happiness: behind the agonizing body the happy soul. So now we had two shaykhs who had descended simultaneously. 'Abd al-Radi was fully upright. The eyes were absent and half-closed. 'Abd al-Radi with his ghost rider Bakhit did not seem quite the equal of the continuously singing old man. He remained in his posture, upright on his knees, his eyes half-closed, his countenance was pale, his breathing consisted of soft snorts and gurgles. From time to time he exclaimed, "All Muslims bless the Prophet." He was gruff with the other possessed man. Then he made attempts to prophesy. The old man continued to sing with a transfigured face. 'Abd al-Radi extended his hand in the direction of the old man, as if he wanted to hold him. He made a gesture, probably a very controlled gesture, as if he wanted to hit him. He tried again to reach out toward the old man and finally felt his head. But the old man turned further away, still singing, and evaded 'Abd al-Radi's hand. Finally he himself stopped singing and turning. He exhaled the air out with one sharp breath, *sss*. The torso gave way a little, pushed back by the recoil. The shaykh had left him. The possessed 'Abd al-Radi was visibly pleased. He prophesied for a while in a loud voice, then suddenly and unexpectedly he fell back and greeted his guest with a distraught, tired look. Then for a while the conversation turned around this and that: An old seal, found in a field, was examined. It was thought to belong to an unknown man, probably long since dead.

The incense burning was renewed as the embers were no longer glowing. 'Abd al-Radi again fell into a state of possession, and wanted to drink in the incense; he threw the incense pot on the straw mat, so that the glowing embers had to be swept away, and grumbled. It seems that not enough incense had been prepared. More was brought. The incense fumes again rose up. 'Abd al-Radi took the pot and drank his fill of the incense. The old man reached curiously for the pot. 'Abd al-Radi—now in the person of Bakhit—prevented him from doing this with the unpleasant laugh. Finally the old man got hold of the pot and was enraptured. He took a glowing ember, and chewed on it so that sparks fell from his mouth. His lips were covered with the spittle, blackened by the ember that dribbled down to his chin and beard. He reached out his hand to me. I gave him my hand. He pulled me close to him and sang. After a minute or two he dropped my hand. People said he wanted my *riha*. I rolled up two piasters in my handkerchief. 'Abd al-Radi's attendants said, "Give the *riha* to Bakhit, he is the master of this place, he will give it to the Abbadi." Bakhit received the *riha*, felt the money, and did not want to pass the handkerchief on. I gently took it back from him and tossed it to the Abbadi. He picked it up, felt the money, and immediately without hesitation tossed it back. I gave Bakhit the *riha* again, so he could remove the money. He took the money with a sour laugh. The Abbadi sobered up without special signs, retreated to the corner, and wrapped his headcloth again. He picked up a *tar*, a hand drum, began to beat it, and endlessly sang his song in a monotonous undertone.

The next day I was supposed to see the old man again as he wanted to tell my fortune. But 'Abd al-Radi's attendants had made it clear to him that he had better travel on.

Personally Received Messages as Illustrations of the Clairvoyance of the Possessed

'Abd al-Radi's significance for his countrymen lies in the circumstances that he became first of all a door between the world of the dead and the living, and secondly that the one who opened the door, the ghostly spirit Bakhit, can provide information about the distant and the hidden.

This clairvoyance encompasses two areas: The ghost Bakhit can have insight into the unspoken thoughts of a visitor, as if he can see into men from above as one would look into a pot; moreover, he can see situations and events that are unknown to the visitor himself.

Bakhit the ghost requires a stimulus in order to infer these pictures and provide this performance. If the visitor wishes information about a circumstance that is important to him, such as a trip and its chances of success, it is enough for him to take 'Abd al-Radi's hand when he is possessed by Bakhit. However, if one wants to learn something about another person or an animal, then he must put something into the hand of the possessed that was in physical contact with this person or animal, for instance, a thread or scrap of a robe, a sweaty cap, a couple of hairs from an animal's tail. This token is called *riha* (scent, pl. *riyah*). The possessed one holds this sample in his hand, and by touching it there appears in the sight of the ghost the person, animal, or situation which is invoked here; and furthermore, the ghost sees this person or animal in causal interconnection with its past and future, so that he can advise how to act in order to achieve a good outcome.

This clairvoyance is however sometimes obscured. Sometimes the expected picture does not appear at all in the sight of the ghost, who thus can only provide erroneous or incomplete information. We can probably estimate that half the information provided is unsatisfactory. But the other half of the information is true, often at first sight amazingly accurate. And in order to reach this truth the fellah patiently and forgivingly accepts the false information into the bargain. If the information were without exception, or mostly, erroneous, then after a week no one would bring a *riha* or a small gift for the shaykh. The fellah is a natural skeptic, above all when it comes to handing over money.

We will examine later the content of the prophecies requested by the peasants. In order to give a picture of the level of clairvoyance of the possessed, I will report the messages that were given to me, and which I can thus evaluate directly.

My case was certainly a special one. I am a European; the ghost Bakhit thus had to receive his images from a world strange to him. One of the repeated questions once put Bakhit ill at ease. He sketched with his hand two parallel straight lines before him and stammered something about the difference of religion, *adyan*, that is between Christianity and Islam, and about the great distance that separated him from my homeland. The parallel lines indicated that religious, as much as spatial, boundaries were hard for him to overcome. Secondly, I did not come to him with a burning concern, as most of his visitors did: The emotional stimulus that the questioner probably brings to the topic of the question because of his own thoughts, and which he lets work on the ghost, was also much smaller. Thirdly, compared to the modest gifts of the fellahin my presents to the ghost were considerable—the anticipation of this might have been a disturbing factor that might have complicated the process of finding the right image. Finally, my visits were more frequent than those of other advice-seekers, even though I had no special reasons to seek out the clairvoyant. Thus the same images, once found, recurred to the clairvoyant, a kind of repertory came into being, which was then available to the ghost in response to each inquiry.

I must say a few words about my personal circumstances in order to characterize the thought construction in which the clairvoyant had to find his way.

I live on the edge of the city of Tübingen. My modest but modern house stands in a small garden. The house door opens onto a path that leads directly to the garden gate, and so to the street. There are no buildings on the opposite side of the street; instead there is a meadow with apple trees, on a hillside. I had left my wife and my son, then aged ten years, and my four-year-old daughter in this house. I came to Cairo in October 1933. I lived there for two months with a German painter I had befriended. I was looking for interest and support to carry out an ambitious multi-year project to investigate Egyptian ethnography. When this goal proved unattainable, I traveled in early December to Kiman, in order to clarify certain questions of ethnography, especially concerning the technology of rope-making, knotting, basketry, and spinning. The amount of time I would stay in Kiman and any further possibilities for research were not yet settled.

I visited 'Abd al-Radi for the first time on December 10. As he was entering into possession and Bakhit appeared in him, I gave him my handkerchief as a *riha*. My thoughts *(damir)* were on the well-being of my wife and children. He began to speak of a forthcoming trip—by railroad *pff pff pff*—southward. He clapped his hands together twice, twice ten, twenty days—in twenty days there will be a trip. The children were characterized by hand as being smaller and larger, then he raised two fingers and wiggled them emphatically back and forth: two children. He moved his hand up and down—the children are playing ball—he holds both hands one over the other, fingers to the mouth—they are playing the flute. Then he characterized my wife, raised his hands to the level of his cheeks, presumably to indicate long hair, and stroked his robe softly to indicate beautiful, respectable clothing.

The statements were accurate. I did indeed travel southward about twenty days later on a short visit to Luxor. My son played the flute frequently in those days.

It is possible that 'Abd al-Radi knew of my family relationships from earlier visits. I had arrived in Kiman only a few days earlier, and the people of Naj' al-Hijayri had very little interest in my personal circumstances. But the possibility of an earlier orientation of 'Abd al-Radi exists, because I had hired a lad from this village as a servant in spring 1932.

I visited him again the next day, December 11. The discovery of the previous day—two children—was immediately brought up again, but this time with further details—the older child is a boy, the younger one a girl. I would spend nineteen days in Kiman, then five in Luxor. I wanted to learn if my friend the painter from Cairo would visit me as expected. With this thought in mind, I took 'Abd al-Radi's hand. He immediately made a sign, and pointed toward the north, "come here"— someone with whom I had been was coming—a woman? No, a man—we would travel away together—far away—across the sea and mountains— until we reached home. In a later possession moment on the same day I wanted to learn something about a friend from my youth who had disappeared four years previously. With this in mind I took 'Abd al-Radi's hand. The ghost was not at all able to find the key. He clung to what he already knew, two children, a wife, someone coming.

The information that the stay in Luxor would last five days was wrong. I was only there for a day. My thoughts of the painter in Cairo were seen correctly by the ghost. No one knew that I was waiting for someone. But the information proved wrong: The painter did not come, nor did I travel back to Germany with him.

On the afternoon of December 24, Bakhit's ghost advised me in general that my wife and children were well. A man—I was still thinking of the painter—would come in fifteen days.

After visiting 'Abd al-Radi I went for a walk in the nearby desert. As I was enjoying the coming of the night in the open air by myself, a man came riding a donkey from Naj' al-Hijayri, looking for me. There was a telegram for me. I returned and stopped for a moment to visit 'Abd al-Radi. The messenger had first looked for me there, so 'Abd al-Radi knew that a telegram had come for me. Entering immediately into possession, the spirit Bakhit announced a vague link between the man who was coming and the telegram. Not that night, but early the next morning the man would arrive by train *pff pff pff*. We would depart together after fifteen days.

I had also thought the telegram might be from the painter. Perhaps this thought had become accessible to the ghost. However, the telegram was a Christmas greeting from my wife. The painter did not come the next day, or ever. And instead of the announced fifteen days, I stayed three more months in Kiman.

On December 25 in the morning I visited 'Abd al-Radi again. Among the guests of the shaykh was also the messenger who had informed me of the arrival of the telegram the day before. He had walked me home, so that he could earn a handsome tip in case the telegram brought good news. He had learned that the telegram was from my wife. Doubtless he had mentioned this to 'Abd al-Radi. 'Abd al-Radi fell into possession and now announced that the telegram was from my wife. He made up for this naïve and cheap message by another in the same sitting, which was certainly the best one that I received from the clairvoyant. I held out my hand to the possessed 'Abd al-Radi, to learn something about my family; in particular I was thinking of the image of my little daughter under the Christmas tree. First the seer prophesied in vague snippets something about my wife, then using gestures he clearly indicated the smaller of the two children. He then took the incense pot in both hands, horizontally, and rocked it back and forth, and said, "carriage." The older child is walking next to the smaller one.

'Abd al-Radi had never in his life seen a doll's carriage. The fellahin have no idea about either a child's or a doll's carriage. The thought lies very distant. The gesture—taking the pot by its handles with both hands at once, and then articulating the word "carriage" made the image unambiguous. I had no idea what my wife would give the children for Christmas, I had not even thought about it, and least of all had I imagined a doll carriage. After a while my wife wrote me that she had given the child a doll carriage, and that she had been very happy with it.

On January 1, 1934, the ghost Bakhit told me that I would receive a letter from the "government" which would tell me to stay in Egypt. The letter would not come soon but after a while. I asked, "Shaykh Bakhit, how long will I stay here?" He showed two fingers, then three—three months. "Three months, or three weeks or . . . ?" Three months. Tomorrow you will get a letter from your wife. She is well, so are the children. The children are playing with the doll carriage and the flute.

On that day I had not been thinking at all about my future and important letters, although admittedly I had been doing so on the previous days. That I might stay for a lengthy period in Kiman—without any specification of time—is something I might have mentioned to the old Sanusi, my landlord. An influence on 'Abd al-Radi through a corresponding comment of my assistant, Mahdi, Sanusi's son, is not likely but possible. The information of the clairvoyant was accurate. The letter, offering me the means for my now reduced research plans, came later from the German Emergency Research Fund. After exactly three months I left Kiman for a trip throughout Egypt. The promise of a letter from my wife on the following day proved wrong.

On January 10, I hoped for information through 'Abd al-Radi on an expected transmission of money from Cairo. Bakhit's ghost recounted that my wife was being visited by another woman and that they were talking about me. Then he prophesied about a man who would soon come and with whom I would travel further. His letter is on the way. I took his hand again to help him find the key. In vain. His messages followed the usual imagery of the playing children, reassured me that they were well, and ended with the recent revelation—the letter from the "government" that would instruct me to stay in Egypt. From time to time he made the sign of paying money.

The visit to my wife is too general and too obvious to be tested as a performance and then taken into account. Furthermore, the revelations are drawn together from different sessions. My thoughts, for which I had come, were not discovered.

On January 18, I went to 'Abd al-Radi to hear something about the health of my wife, who had complained of eye trouble in a letter. The possessed one spoke first of a man who had something to do with the "government." This man received appreciatively a letter in which I reported my research on rope-making and basketry in Kiman. Then he prophesied more about a man who would come soon—I would stay here another month. Then he invoked an open area where my children would be playing—"See, see, I see them"—he pointed northwest with his hand; his sight was completely blank. He made very lively motions of playing ball. "Now the mother hits the children because they don't want to come," he made the customary gesture of hitting. "Now the children are eating from plates and drinking. The woman is reading a letter from you," and he made the gesture of reading. But the clairvoyant did not react to my concern about the health of my wife's eyes. Finally I asked about it. Then he responded that her eyes were healthy, although my wife was wearing glasses.

The letter speaking of rope-making I had actually written to Professor Littmann.[6] And precisely in those days my letter should have been in his hands. The man about to come is a holdover from earlier oracles, when I was expecting a visit from the painter. This image now had a secure place in the repertory. The images of the household life of the children and the reading woman are remarkable for their liveliness. My wife's eye problems were minimized, and in any case she did not wear glasses.

On January 25, the clairvoyant portrayed first of all from the repertory, gradually becoming boring, of children playing ball. "Now the ball has fallen into the water, another child fetches it—now they are

---

6 Enno Littman (1875–1958), German Orientalist, professor in Tübingen since 1921, who continued to support Winkler after 1933 by helping him find research funding. NSH

playing with the doll carriage—now the children are eating—everyone is cheerful—your wife's eyes are exceptionally healthy." Then he surprised me: "A man is coming, and another with him." He looked, and pointed north, adding the man is not coming here, he would write me, come to see me. I would visit him.

Two days earlier I had learned that Herr Littmann was coming to Cairo with his spouse. I had not mentioned this expectation to anyone. In fact, this letter soon came, inviting me to visit him, and I did go to Cairo to see the Littmanns.

On February 15 I visited 'Abd al-Radi without the intention of consulting a ghost spirit. Perhaps because he hoped for a present which Bakhit, and not 'Abd al-Radi, would receive, he had the incense pot brought, fell quickly into possession and began to present prophecies on a desert trip that I would make in a southeasterly direction. I would ride on a camel, and a man would walk next to me. Then he awoke from the possession, but after a very short break sank into another. Now he brought forth his usual repertory—wife and children. This time, however, he described the home: "It sits in a garden, on a street, across from the garden gate are trees—banana trees—near the house is a pump from which much water flows—in the open space between the house door and the garden gate the boy slides quickly back and forth—the woman sits in a room ('Abd al-Radi demonstrated the European way of sitting by drawing his knees up) and reads. Now the children are near the mother, playing and laughing *krr krr*." He also announced that I had received a package from my wife containing something to eat.

I did not have the desert trip in mind when I gave the shaykh my *riba*; however, in the previous days I had been thinking about the trip a lot. I was going to make a camel trip during which I planned to search for rock drawings and inscriptions in the desert. Shortly after this session I made this trip, but with two camels for me and the accompanying guide. The depiction of the house is accurate. The banana trees *(moz)* are noteworthy, perhaps coming through confusion with *loz* (almond trees). Our apple trees are unknown to a good Qift fellah, and he might have seen them as almond trees. Especially remarkable is the pump near the house, for in reality there was none at all. We will see later how this pump got into the picture, when we examine the relationships between 'Abd al-Radi's waking and dream consciousness. The image of the boy sliding between the house door and the garden gate is also noteworthy. I did not check whether at that time my son had laid out a sledding path in this place, certainly suitable for one. It is possible. Such a winter sport is naturally completely unimaginable to a fellah, and so as a performance of intuition is not without weight. I had in fact received a package of cookies from my wife.

I went to 'Abd al-Radi on March 2. I asked almost immediately why I was not receiving any letters. "A letter is coming by airplane, and is late because of the exceptionally bad weather." Then the family life in detail was depicted. My wife is reading—many people are there—the children are playing ball. In a few strokes he laid out before himself the situation of the house—the street here—the garden with the trees there. No mention this time of the pump.

I occasionally received air-mail letters, and in winter the air mail is not at all regular, and all of this I had explained to 'Abd al-Radi from time to time. I did not note whether an air mail letter came at this time.

On March 11, I visited 'Abd al-Radi shortly before my departure the next day on my desert trip. The seer promised me a beautiful find—three rock walls, in the right corner of which, crowded together, would be pictures and inscriptions, somewhere to the north of the desert road from Qift to the Red Sea. Then followed the unavoidable description of the reading woman and the playing children, the house, the street, and the garden. The pump is now back in the picture and is in full use.

The inscription discovery was correctly intuited. The depiction of the three rock faces north of the road could apply to a couple of locations, but most of all to the first, most impressive, delightful, and informative spot.

On March 25, I consulted 'Abd al-Radi in possession for the last time. He sketched out in the usual way the idyllic family and provided details on the house and its situation. Noteworthy and important for our later examination of 'Abd al-Radi's soul is the addition, next to the house and the puzzling pump, of a dovecote. "The pigeons fly and coo around the home, *kukukuku*." Moreover, near the house one finds a railroad.

The actual house has neither pump nor dovecote. The railroad is at least a kilometer away, but there is a light railway a couple of hundred meters away that connects a clay pit to a brick factory.

The Impact of the Possessed
on the Religious and Social Life
of the Fellahin

'Abd al-Radi's Situation in the Eyes of the Fellahin

When 'Abd al-Radi first began to display the characteristic traits of possession—running into the desert and hitting himself, then returning home with a vacant look, and speaking as another, as a stranger to his own people in obscure language—his relatives thought he had gone crazy, *majnun*. The phrase *majnun* lacks the polished, cool meaning of our words 'crazy' or 'mad.' The Upper Egyptian fellah is too close to demons to interpret a spiritual disturbance just as a matter of mental disturbance, a confusion of the real, a delusion or a hollow deception. If he calls a mentally ill person *majnun*, this can only be taken to mean 'possessed by *jinn*' (demons). And a fellah would never be able to free himself from the horror of the demonic when dealing with a fool, no matter how bizarre. We saw above (p. 81) that the attendants of 'Abd al-Radi sought to expel the supposed demons, and how they were taught that a ghost had selected him as a mount. They let themselves be persuaded, and now think that the ghost 'clothes' *(libis)* himself with the body of 'Abd al-Radi. During this 'clothing' 'Abd al-Radi's soul is 'absent, hidden' *(ghayib)*. And since during the possession moments it is not 'Abd al-Radi but Bakhit who is present, people greet the eruption of ghostly possession as that of an arriving guest: "Welcome, Bakhit."

A ghost is frightening for the one who is seized, and frightening for the relatives, whom he threatens with illness and death in order to force the accomplishment of his wishes. Outsiders are left in peace. The ghost of Bakhit conceived a love for 'Abd al-Radi, which is why he descends on him, and in order to provide the daily bread, speaks through the mouth of 'Abd al-Radi, who receives the honoraria for this. So Bakhit appears as a businessman and is treated as such by the clients. The quality of the relationship between the fellahin seeking advice and Bakhit is often quite businesslike. Bakhit wants payment for his messages, and the client wants answers for his money. We have reported how regular contracts are negotiated between a ghost from Bakhit's crew and the clients (see p. 88). It can happen that Bakhit scolds the client the way an army doctor does a contrary patient or a judge a stubborn defendant. And the client presses Bakhit, and not infrequently, when the prophetic process is not working. "Speak Arabic," said one cross fellah in a session to Bakhit, when Bakhit did not know what to say to him and stalled him with obscure scraps and gestures. While the tone is businesslike, the partners are not on equal ground, for Bakhit is always the superior. The fellah comes to him with the feeling with which he would seek out a not ill-disposed village chief. If he gets angry with Bakhit, he would not say it to his face; at most he would curse him on the way home with the customary "May God curse your father." But he runs the risk that Bakhit, with his ability to see and hear at a distance, would perceive this and throw it back at him in a later consultation, with an embarrassing uproar.

Now of course the appearance of a ghost runs straight against all Islamic speculation on the fate of the dead person. The fellah is a pious Muslim. He does not know the teaching and speculations of Muslim scholars on the fate of the dead in the period between death and resurrection. But what the Prophet Muhammad revealed and preached as essential is the foundation of his soul—trust in the merciful Lord of the Worlds. And on this foundation there is room enough for ghosts who hover around and reveal themselves. Of course there are also 'scholars' in the villages—scholars in a sense different from ours. These are people who can read and write, who have learned this skill from the revealed word of the Qur'an and essentially only because of the Qur'an. These people now observe how 'Abd al-Radi enters into possession, how another speaks through him, someone who has legitimized himself as a Muslim, and is blessed with clairvoyance—and this other in 'Abd al-Radi claims to be the ghost of a person known to all, and can call forth a whole row of similar ghosts. The easy answer, to call all this cheating and swindling, does not occur to them, for it is not charlatanry. Another explanation they can easily evoke is that an evil demon among the *jinn* has entered into 'Abd al-Radi; but this is not possible either, since the ghost shows that it is devout and good. So the only remaining solution is to take the ghost for a *jinn*, but for a believing and pious one. Muhammad had already allowed room in his message for believing demons. And this pious *jinn* likes to show himself in the mask of Bakhit and other departed ones. This is then the meaning that the village scholars have of 'Abd al-Radi and his ghosts, and many non-learned fellahin also follow this interpretation, including some women peasants. They say, "*Ma fish mashayikh,*" there are no ghosts.

The Possessed as Spokesman for the Dead

We have already met the most unsettling effect of 'Abd al-Radi on the fellahin when observing the ghosts who appear in him. Many departed persons utilize this door to the world of the living in order to speak to their relatives. The reasons for this appearance are several.

Suddenly torn from life, Muhammad 'Abd al-Qadir of Barahma came to reassure his parents, to tell them that he was taken from the world by the will of God, because of an accident in the material world; he came to ask them not to weep for him any more because their tears hurt his cheeks.

Other ghosts, such as 'Ali from Barahma and Nur al-Din from 'Aqula, are driven by concern for their orphans in the world of the living. They afflicted their fathers with illness when they saw that they acted badly with the grandchildren left behind, and obliged leniency and fair behavior.

Still others, such as Khalifa Mustafa from al-Shaykhiya and Muhammad Ahmad from al-Qal'a, appear to order the construction of a memorial tomb on earth.

These ghosts are frightening because of their demands and because of their power to send illness and death if no one listens to them.

We can draw several conclusions from this material. Unjust behavior toward orphans can lead to the anger of the dead parents, and in anger the ghosts can send sickness. Sins and sickness imply each other, as in the beliefs of so many people. Moreover, we can underline the strongly felt wish of the dead, as in ancient Egypt, to leave a memorial on earth.

The Possessed as Advisor in Illness

Ghosts can send illness. So those who are afflicted turn to a medium who mediates ghosts, so that the unfortunate can be heard and reconciled. Moreover, any fellah would prefer to go to a possessed person or to a magician to cure his illness rather than to a doctor. First of all, the doctor charges too much. But there is more: The fellah does not trust the doctor. The modern doctor does not have the same relationship as the fellah to illness. In the consciousness of the fellahin rules above all the thought that God is the cause of all that happens; this can lead to a lazy and mindless fatalism, but it can to the same degree teach an unshakable serenity in life. I have heard from pious fellahin with a severe illness, "This is not my affair, but a matter for the Lord God." For such pious people, prayer and alms are the only way to seek healing. For a ghost to appear and transmit clairvoyant information and advice is somehow a grace from God. So it is natural that when an ill person turns to someone possessed, even when he does not hold the ghost responsible for his illness, he sees that person as sent by God. The ghosts are between the living and God, but they are nearer to God than to people, which may make them able somehow to help from the far side, whose finality is God.

In the following we will enumerate some cures and treatments that Bakhit prescribed while in a state of possession.

Once 'Abd al-Radi recognized from a *riha* that a women was having urinary difficulties. He prescribed a decoction of different herbs, with an emphasis on *karawiya*, wild caraway.

A sick child received a prescription to drink lots of water. In many such cases of illness Bakhit recommended to the parent to direct his walk to the desert and to seek there the herb *'atni* (*Daemin tomentosa* (L.) Vatke) and to swab the whole body with its caustic milk. This milk causes inflammations, which are supposed to be good for cleansing the blood.

A sulfur ointment was prescribed for a sick buffalo cow.

In the case of another sick buffalo cow 'Abd al-Radi determined that the animal had been struck by the evil eye. The owner of the cow should take an egg from an old hen, set light to a cow patty, place the egg in the smoke, and then break the egg on the embers. Then he should pour salt water down the cow's throat. If it is God's wish, the cow will recover.

Once a brown, somewhat black youth with a sad appearance presented a bit of cloth as *riha*. Bakhit quickly found the clue. The *riha* came from the youth's brother, who had sent it to him from Qusayr, the port on the Red Sea. Bakhit spoke of the desert mountains in which the owner of the *riha* had once spent the night. A block of stone fell, and gave him a fright that now made him ill. The symptoms of the illness were very generally described by 'Abd al-Radi as pain in the area of the heart, the stomach, and the legs. In order to recover, the brother should prepare a tea from *rawand* (rhubarb), squeeze into it the juice of a lemon, and then drink this tea on an empty stomach every morning for seven days. On the seventh day he should cook a pigeon without any other ingredients in lemon juice, consume it, and drink the juice. If God wills, this will help. In addition, the sick boy should have an *'ugad* prepared by him, Bakhit. We will shortly see what an *'ugad* is.[7]

Another sent his brother a *riha* from Isma'iliya. Bakhit found out that the man had been struck by the evil eye. Again he prescribed lemons as a cure. The lad who brought the *riha* had already visited Bakhit once. At that time Bakhit advised him to have an *'ugad* prepared. So the youth this time produced the material for one, and gave it to Bakhit—an iron ring the size of a finger ring, and with it a bunch of cotton yarn. Bakhit divided the yarn, took about half of it and tore it off. He put this half under the mat as a little extra on the honorarium. He rolled up the other half quickly on his thigh, so that the threads were all wound together. Then he tied the resulting skein to the ring with a knot, then tightly next to this knot a second, a third, and so on, until all the metal of the ring was covered. During this process, he whispered continually and tensely, probably pious blessings and sayings. When he had completed his task, he tightened the open end of the skein to cover the ring, tied it tight, and let the very end of the thread hang

---

7 Literally, 'knots.' NSH

freely, so that one could now attach the talisman to the body. To finish it off, Bakhit kissed the *'ugad* in order to transmit to it more blessings, and gave it to the boy for his brother, with instructions to carry this on the right side of the chest.

This then is an *'ugad* (see illustration). Such knotted rings were also prepared by other possessed mediums, so this is not at all unique to Bakhit. Bakhit likes to prescribe this for all possible occasions, certainly not without thinking of the extra bit of yarn, which his "camel" on occasion tucks away. The solemn process of knotting also impresses the guests.

The Case of 'Abbas

One day I heard that a new ghost had descended and seized a person. I learned this a few days after the event. This newly possessed person was treated in a variety of ways. He was also taken to 'Abd al-Radi. To learn how possession begins in its first stages was of the greatest interest to me, not least in order to see how 'Abd al-Radi would react to this comrade in fate.

I have already often mentioned this possessed person in this book. This is 'Abbas, the brother of Fatma with the beautiful eyes who sits on the path to Qift, 'Abbas, the same one for whose recovery the Shaziliya *zikr* was performed, which I attended (pp. 61–62), the same one for whom the whole team of ghosts appeared in 'Abd al-Radi when he was consulted (p. 100).

This is what I was able to learn about 'Abbas. He came from the "family of camel drivers," honest, upright people from the village of 'Awadat near Qift. His father died when he was still a small boy. He had only a somewhat older sister, Shaykha Fatma. In the spring of 1934, 'Abbas was about twenty years old. His mother was blind; the pock-marked haggard face of the poor old woman showed that smallpox had destroyed her sight. When the children were still young and she was overburdened with cares, she made a vow to Shaykh Ansari that she would bring him a sacrifice if she was able to raise her son to adulthood. The woman had not yet made good on this vow, although the youth had reached adulthood some time ago.

'Abbas worked as a day laborer for peasants and as a *sabakh*, a digger of saltpeter clay. One day, a few days before I knew of this, 'Abbas was in the desert with his donkey, loading up sacks with this clay. A shaykh, a ghost, grabbed him there. Trembling, distraught, feverish, and exhausted, he returned home. In the night he saw many people coming to him, who knelt on him. He called out, horrified, "*Nas, nas,*" ("people, people"). Then he saw one of these people, who was aiming a shotgun at him. He was terribly afraid. In this fantasy he called out two names, Ahmad and Mahmud. His friends, who were keeping vigil over their ill comrade, looked at each other—those must be the names of the ghosts who had seized him out there in the desert. Also the people who were kneeling on him and shooting at him were assumed to be ghosts, *mashayikh*. By the next day the situation had not changed at all. He still kept referring to Mahmud in his confused speech, interrupted by pious formulae, and called himself *tahrir* (pure, chaste). No one knew which Mahmud he was referring to. His speech was confused, the signs too few—it could also be that a *jinn*, a demon, had entered into him. They burned rags under his nose, in order to exorcise the possible *jinn* or *shaytan*. In vain. They invited a man who knew the Qur'an to recite over him. He whispered the profession of faith into his ear. 'Abbas repeated this out loud with difficulty, and added "I am not a *shaytan*, a devil." People did not know what to do next. They locked him into his home. The next day they let him out. He wanted to run to the desert hills. Naturally he was prevented from going. But five men took him to see 'Abd al-Radi in Naj' al-Hijayri. 'Abd al-Radi was then saying the afternoon prayers, and then entered into his *khilwa* and awaited the descent of Bakhit. First of all al-Asyuti appeared and sang his praises of the eternal. Then Bakhit appeared, felt the head and body of 'Abbas, and said, "People think there is a *shaytan* in him, but it is a shaykh who descended on him, a big shaykh. For this reason 'Abbas will never marry." Then Bakhit scolded one of the men accompanying 'Abbas, "Why are you hitting 'Abbas? He is a shaykh. Why did you burn rags under his nose?" My assistant Mahdi was one of those accompanying him. As a literate person he dared to ask again the question whether a devil might not have entered into 'Abbas. Bakhit gave a clear answer, "No, no, it is not a devil. These are *mashayikh*, ghosts. Shaykh Mahmud has his nose, and Shaykh Ahmad has taken his right side." That ghostly seizures begin on the right side is something 'Abd al-Radi had felt in his own body. Bakhit now signaled in the air, "Let him go, Mahmud, he is a poor fellah." Then Bakhit prescribed that 'Abbas should be bathed with the leaves of the lotus tree, dressed in a clean white robe, that a *khilwa* should be set up, a place to convey oracles, then the shaykh would descend on him. Furthermore, the sacrificial offering that 'Abbas's mother had promised must be brought to Shaykh Ansari. Then everyone recited the *Fatiha* on Bakhit's orders. 'Abbas went home with his companions, supposedly improved.

I have to thank my assistant Mahdi for this report. He also told me that 'Abbas's mother had seen Shaykh Ansari in a dream the night after the first possession. He said to her, "Didn't you once make me a vow on behalf of your son?" In the dream the mother promised to fulfill the vow.

In the meantime people were speaking of this case around Qift. The government doctor heard of it, and had 'Abbas brought to the quarantine tents outside the city, which had coincidentally been set up to isolate suspected smallpox victims.

As soon as I heard the news of this new possession case, I went to the quarantine station to see for myself. This was Monday, February 19. Here again I follow the notes I entered into my diary that give my first impressions.

At the edge of Qift the quarantine tents had been installed, separated from the houses by the now empty bed of a canal. On the Qift side a good crowd had gathered; people were standing and squatting around and observing the other side, where 'Abbas the newly possessed stood alone in front of a tent. I went across and greeted him—a brown-skinned, clearly black lad, froth at the corners of his mouth and on his lips. His face was twisted with resigned pain. His knees trembled. He was holding crushed breadcrumbs in his hand. Then later he pulled lumps of clay from his pocket. A relative, who had come with me, said that he would eat such lumps of clay. The relative wiped the dried spittle from his mouth. He gave a very pitiful impression. He recognized me from the street. He also recognized others who were asking him questions. His speech was slurred, unclear. Occasionally he stopped at a word, painstakingly looking for the right syllables. He spoke something about shoes treading on the grave of Mahmud. He kept repeating, stammering, that he was Muslim. Islam is also for him the refuge in the depths of his soul. He frequently spoke the name of Mahmud, then he stretched himself, his eyes blinked faster, and with a clear, excited voice he called out this name. A crowd of people came with me and his relative, and the orderly from time to time chased them away. 'Abbas himself turned on a gang of curious children who had gathered around. People thought that probably somewhere, along the path to the market, there must once have been the grave of Mahmud. And now Mahmud is insulted because this spot, sacred to him, is desecrated by the shoes of those taking the path. After a while, the young doctor came, and I arranged an appointment with him.

Returning to the village I passed the simple-minded sister of 'Abbas. She sat all huddled up in the shade of a house. She had laid her head on her thigh and stared vacantly in front of her. I greeted her. She slowly lifted up her torso and head and looked at me with beautiful, deeply sad, and distant eyes. "Don't be afraid," I said. Slowly her facial expression turned to crying. She was crying because of "yesterday," because of her brother.

I did not see 'Abbas the next day. My assistant Mahdi reported that 'Abbas's mother had sold a pair of chickens in the market and had gotten a billy goat to offer as a sacrifice to Shaykh Ansari. The mother had also gotten some white cloth to make the robe for her son that Bakhit had prescribed. 'Abbas had been released by the doctor. Mahdi had seen him in front of his house in a happy mood. He had a whip in his hand and was imagining that he would chase the sparrows away from a field. He was cracking the whip and calling out a frightening call, "*haha.*" His sister Fatma, whom I found very depressed the day before, was merry today, sitting next to her brother, who was chasing away imaginary birds, and laughing at the scene.

I spoke to the doctor soon afterward. He had been unable to reach a satisfactory diagnosis. Since 'Abbas had not committed any violence, since they could not help him, and since the doctor was anyway very much in demand, he released him. His relatives were pleased to have him back. In order to keep him out of the doctor's way, they took him to an uncle in a somewhat distant village. However, they brought him back again after a few days.

I then saw 'Abbas for the second time. On my way to the post office I caught sight of Fatma. The girl was laughing and signaled to me awkwardly. She said happily that 'Abbas had returned. He was sitting on the other side of the street with his cousin, a grocer. He was holding a piece of sugar cane. This, and his face, were black with flies. He greeted me with a pious phrase. His voice was a little tense, shaky, and close to tears. His whole body seemed to be trembling. He put words together with hesitation and difficulty. He interpreted his circumstances as sent by God. He showed me a red banner, which apparently was intended for the coming new Shaykh Mahmud.

The next day I saw him again. He was sitting next to his sister. The two together—double misery. In one hand he was holding crushed breadcrumbs and half a piaster, in the other a piece of bread. When I began to speak to him, he began to cry. The blind old mother of the pair told me that the next evening there would be a sacrifice and a *zikr* for 'Abbas and that I should come.

I have already reported on my visit to this *zikr* (p. 62).

The *zikr* did not help 'Abbas very much. On Sunday, March 4, in the afternoon my assistant Mahdi told me that 'Abbas was about to pass by. He was on his way to Naj' al-Hijayri to see 'Abd al-Radi. Then he arrived, in a white robe, with a red and white head cloth that hung down to his shoulders, and he had a piece of sugar cane in his hand. Behind him came his blind mother, led by an old man. Shortly after 'Abbas passed by, I started off. I now follow my diary.

I caught up with him on the way. In Naj' al-Hijayri we waited in 'Abd al-Radi's vestibule. Two donkeys were rolling around in the dust and stirring up terrible clouds. 'Abd al-Radi had gone to say his afternoon prayers in the mosque. He came back shortly. He was unusually serious, almost grim. After a brief, conventionally hearty greeting, 'Abd al-Radi entered his *khilwa* and sat in his place, with us around him. I suspected that 'Abd al-Radi was so serious and even upset because of 'Abbas—perhaps he feared a rival. The incense pot was brought. 'Abd al-Radi breathed in fumes, then grabbed the pot and drank in the smoke avidly. He was fully upright on his knees. Twice he raised the pot and held it for a long time in front of his face, then he tossed it away. A few whiffs of smoke reached 'Abbas, who began hesitantly to breathe it in, then soon stopped. There were still a few people there awaiting messages from Bakhit. Bakhit advised them, then turned to 'Abbas.

Then a remarkable succession of ghostly spirits appeared one after the other. I have already reported this (pp. 100f.). It seemed as if 'Abd al-Radi was using this full complement of ghosts to feel his way with respect to the newly possessed. There appeared Shaykh 'Ali, al-Asyuti, Wardani, 'Abd al-Qadir al-Jilani, Salim al-Huwi, and in between them Bakhit, then Muhammad Ahmad from al-Qal'a, who greeted them, his parents being present among the clients, along with his cousin, who reached two agreements. 'Abd al-Radi awoke from his possession, after a short pause fell into a new one, and then Bakhit appeared and finally turned to the case of 'Abbas.

During the whole time 'Abbas was sitting before 'Abd al-Radi and observed him fearfully yet trustingly. One could easily see that this case of 'Abbas was painful for 'Abd al-Radi, who found the youth unsympathetic. Bakhit through 'Abd al-Radi demanded that 'Abbas recite the profession of faith. 'Abbas obeyed, and in a hesitant manner he managed to do it. Bakhit then affirmed that 'Abbas was improving. In fact, he was quieter than in the early days of the illness, when he was frothing at the mouth and his face was distorted by pain. Bakhit now announced that the forgotten grave of Mahmud lay behind 'Abbas's house. Bakhit gestured in the air—"Mahmud, let the boy go, let him go." Bakhit did not know exactly what to do. Then he asked again for the profession of faith, 'Abbas, intimidated, recited it. When this was done, Bakhit broke out in his ugly laugh, and 'Abbas laughed along, relieved. Bakhit gave a message about the origin of 'Abbas's illness. Ghostly spirits (mashayikh) ride around in the desert. There they came across 'Abbas as he was digging clay fertilizer, and hit him on the head.

Earlier, people had come one more time with 'Abbas to see Bakhit. But I did not learn anything about that visit. Bakhit ordered 'Abbas's supporters to bring hilba (fenugreek), birsim (clover), and vinegar. Bakhit now demanded these ingredients, and got his people to make a paste with them, then add the vinegar. The paste grew cold. Bakhit stirred it with his hand, and beckoned to 'Abbas to come closer. 'Abbas was now very frightened. Bakhit twice took hold of 'Abbas's temples as if to measure them, and squeezed them. Then he unwrapped 'Abbas's headcloth, took two handfuls of the paste, and smeared it over his skull, thickly. Over this he wrapped a cloth. Bakhit then ordered him firmly to keep this compress on for three days, and then to come back again;

he himself would remove it. Moreover, 'Abbas should, in a particular but unspecified night, go to the spot in the desert where the ghosts had attacked him. There he should lie down. To his head, hands, and feet should be attached keys, and the whole should be censed with *jawli*. Furthermore, his whole body should be covered with seeds of all kinds—wheat, barley, sorgo, beans, fenugreek, whatever was available. Then he would recover. Bakhit reported that Shaykh Mahmud was angry because they had not waited with the sacrifice for Ansari: It would have been better to perform it in three weeks. Anyway, Shaykh Mahmud is currently in Aswan. To conclude, Bakhit demanded for his "camel" a *bafta*, an expensive robe, which is quite a high honorarium. The mother's escort pointed out that the family is dirt poor. But Bakhit only gave a shameless laugh. Then he sent 'Abbas out together with his mother and her escort; he told them many times that they should be gone. They left full of worry.

Thereupon, Bakhit gave two messages, one to me, the other to my assistant, both unimportant. Finally 'Abd al-Radi then awoke, totally exhausted, and on awakening recited the second half of the profession of faith in a tone of physical agony. Then he came fully to himself, looked friendlier, and greeted us.

'Abbas was never taken back to Bakhit; certainly the demand for the honorarium scared the people off. The situation of 'Abbas was then for a while rather uncomfortable. He tore his clothes, struck out at people, even hit his mother. His relatives thereupon shackled him. And so shackled he sat next to his sister Fatma. Gradually he become tamer, the shackles were loosened, the hesitant speech became more regular, his reason returned, and after a few weeks he was cheerfully riding his donkey on the road to the desert. Shaykh Mahmud had freed him, had abandoned the plan to descend on him.

The Possessed as Advisor and Arbiter of Legal Matters and Other Social Affairs

We have already taken note of the ability of the possessed as an advisor in legal matters. Muhammad 'Abd al-Qadir, who was run over by a train, appeared through 'Abd al-Radi in order to let his parents know that he died of an accident, not through an attack on his life (p. 76). In this way he freed his parents and his entire family from the duty of blood revenge against a presumed culprit. Other ghosts, such as 'Ali of

Barahma and Nur al-Din from 'Aqula, appeared through 'Abd al-Radi to demand the rights of the orphans they left behind (pp. 98–99). And we hear of the ghost Muhammad Ahmad from al-Qal'a that he wanted to help his cousin get married.

Next to illness, robbery is a major reason why people come to 'Abd al-Radi for information.

Once two old fellahin sat next to 'Abd al-Radi. One was Yusuf, perhaps sixty years old, and the other about fifty. Along with these two had come Mahmud, a bareheaded lad between sixteen and eighteen years old. He was sitting in the dark background. These people had come from Gurna by the desert well Bir 'Ambar.[8] Old Yusuf gave the possessed 'Abd al-Radi three objects as *riha*: a small strip of cloth, a headscarf *shugga*, and a brown homespun fellah coat, *za'but*. 'Abd al-Radi was possessed by Bakhit. He was casting around for some clue. The two older men wanted more detailed information, and were pressuring him. Bakhit answered in a gruff and irritated way, and in any case without being any clearer. He took the coat and pushed it away; he wanted to have it far away. In a loud gruff answer, he turned full face toward old Yusuf, opening his eyes wide with anger. His eyes were cloudy, glazed over. The old man tried to understand Bakhit. It was an affair of theft. These people had already come once before. Yusuf was the victim. He had given a bit of land to a relative, the other man present. But this man harvested a parcel of land that had not been given to him; in other words, he stole the harvest. Then Yusuf reclaimed the field from him. Then, in anger, Mahmud, the son of this relative, stole a cow from Yusuf, took her away, and hid her. But it was possible to recover the cow without scandal. Then someone stole the wheel buckets, made of metal and so fairly expensive, from Yusuf's waterwheel. The thief had used a sickle to cut them loose from the rim of the wheel. Suspicion soon fell on Mahmud. Mahmud denied any involvement. In the previous session about twelve different tokens *(riyah)* from those suspected had been brought to Bakhit. Three times they passed through his hands, and three times he had picked out the *riha* of Mahmud as that of the thief. On this second visit they were going to run the test again.

---

8 This is north of Qift and so not the well-known Gurna near Luxor. NSH

Mahmud sat scowling in the corner; the headscarf among the three objects that were being presented to Bakhit was his. And once again Bakhit picked out the owner of this scarf as an evildoer and a thief. Angrily Bakhit harked back to the earlier visit. He said that in spite of the clear indication from Bakhit, Mahmud still denied the act. Today as then, Mahmud avoided Bakhit and reviled him. Finally Bakhit threw the headscarf angrily to Mahmoud, who took it and morosely wrapped it around his head. Bakhit now recommended that they drop the matter, for the parties were related through marriage. This relationship was clearly indicated by a gesture.

Another time a schoolteacher from Kiman was sitting among the clients, together with some educated friends. After 'Abd al-Radi fell into possession and Bakhit had entered him, the schoolteacher asked him, without a *riha* since in a case like this there was none available, who had broken into the mosque in Kiman. The thief had stolen a pair of candles, which been there for a long time and were cherished, and also an alarm clock. Bakhit was very indignant about such a crime. He said, "Why didn't the thief just steal the shoes of those praying?" By this he meant that would have been a lesser sin than to take something belonging to the mosque. But the teacher was not satisfied with such talk. He asked urgently and pointedly, "Who was the thief?" Bakhit was now cornered. He said there was no need to name him, and hit himself in the eye: God himself would punish him through his eyes. With this answer the teacher left, not very satisfied.

Another time Bakhit was counseling a visitor something about illness, then with "water" he touched on the illness that was really of concern: urinary problems. After he had offered some advice about this affliction, another guest held out to him urgently a *riha*. Here again, Bakhit spoke in his staccato manner something about "water," there was no doubt that he again meant urinary problems. The petitioner said honestly that this was not what he was asking about. Bakhit was somewhat angry, but followed on immediately and with special coaching from the asker found the right path. The man had lost a cow, as Bakhit now recognized. He built the notion of "water" into a new message, insofar as he now announced that the disappearance of the animal had something to do with a drinking trough. This was plausible to the questioner, and he was satisfied with the answer.

Yet another time a young fellah gave his hand to 'Abd al-Radi, possessed by Bakhit. Bakhit spoke at first something about job possibilities. This thought could not have been too far away, as in this place every young man thinks day and night how he can earn a handful of money. "Wait a bit," said Bakhit, and spoke vaguely about a letter that would come, and then of useless talk among people. But the man did not find this a satisfactory answer. He took the hand of the possessed a second time. Bakhit immediately saw things better, and was very disapproving. The man smiled—Bakhit had found his *damir*, his secret thoughts. "Leave this thing. It's enough," said Bakhit. The other guests listened to the words of Bakhit and whispered their suspicions to each other. After the session and well away from 'Abd al-Radi's house I inquired about the real issue involved. The father of the asker had been killed some time ago. It was unclear who was responsible. But suspicion fell on a certain individual. And then people discovered that this one too had been killed. The man who was asking Bakhit might have been the one who had avenged his father. When the police arrested him he was able to provide an alibi, as many people swore that they had seen him in another place at that time. For some reason, which in this obscure story was not very clear, the man was not satisfied with this revenge— perhaps he suspected the involvement of a second person. For that reason on this day he was seeking Bakhit's advice. Bakhit advised him against further killing.

Another time a man with an anxious look sat before the possessed. Bakhit was soon on the right track. Some time ago the police had searched house to house in his village for weapons. The soldiers found an incredibly long knife in his house. The man was tormenting himself with the thought that he might be thrown into prison. Bakhit told him all this and consoled him: He would only have to pay a money fine.

Once Muhammad, the younger son of Sanusi, presented Bakhit with a *riha*. It was a scrap he had secretly torn from the robe of his brother Mahdi. Bakhit immediately figured out it was Mahdi. He said that Mahdi had quarreled with his father. Muhammad told me later that this was true. Bakhit added that the man to whom this *riha* belonged was not quite right in the head. He was bewitched. His wife kept pieces of paper, so that he always and forever would think of her. Muhammad confided in me that perhaps Mahdi's wife had hidden such slips of paper in her braids. She is the daughter of Shaykh Masri, and he is a specialist in such things.

Peace at home and happiness in marriage are often the wish that leads people, especially women, to 'Abd al-Radi. He sees in his clairvoyance what is missing, advises, and prepares many beneficial ring knots (*ugad*) for his clients. The men are likely to come seeking information about employment opportunities.

'Abd al-Radi as a Central Point in Fellahin Society

If we look back, we see for ourselves how the emergence of 'Abd al-Radi in the peasant society of his village and the surrounding villages provoked an important change. It seems as if, in the middle of scattered pieces, suddenly one piece acquired strong magnetism and the other pieces lying around aligned themselves with it. In the midst of a disorganized mass of fellah souls one suddenly stands out, and the others direct their gaze to it—a central point has emerged. It was an unusual pleasure for the scientific observer to see the emergence of this center with his own eyes, and the development of this new, organizing central point.

We note how at first the nearest relatives of 'Abd al-Radi—spouse, brothers, father—orient themselves to this middle point, how then in his home village people begin to notice him and turn to him, how then his fame spreads to the neighboring villages, and from thence the people come to him with their needs, how then finally people from further away, outside this zone, from as far as Qusayr on the Red Sea or Isma'iliya on the Suez Canal, are attracted to send a *riha* to 'Abd al-Radi, in order to seek his advice.

And we can go further. People come to 'Abd al-Radi from the neighboring villages. They often have to wait a long time, for instance, if they arrive during the turn of women to consult the possessed. Then they squat for hours in the shaded forecourt, meet acquaintances, share stories about their illness and other cases, discuss the prices in the market and the habits of a new official, speak of war in faraway lands and of job opportunities in industrial cities—in short, these visits to 'Abd al-Radi lead to the exchange of news, to the chance to agree on a bargain or to prepare a marriage. The most important person, the quiet pole in this gathering of those waiting, is old Hamed, 'Abd al-Radi's father. Probably in the gathering of the waiting women, which I could not observe,

Fatma, 'Abd al-Radi's spouse, plays a corresponding role. So it happens that 'Abd al-Radi's house has become a meeting place, where there is always something interesting for the fellah to hear. Thus many also come here not to consult the possessed but to hear a few bits of news.

Probably the circle of those who consult 'Abd al-Radi will not grow through time, for he is by no means the only possessed clairvoyant in the area. But it is instructive to observe this kernel of a social center in its early growth. Under special circumstances—namely, when a really important person supports this or stands next to it—such a kernel can grow into a powerful political focus.

A Dervish

I often sat with those waiting and listened to their conversations. I also got to know all kinds of people from the neighboring villages. Once a Yemeni dervish came to Naj' al-Hijayri. Such a man of God—or rather, in this case, a boy of God—fit in superbly among 'Abd al-Radi's visitors. I would like to report in more detail on this guest, who made a deep impression on me.

One day, among 'Abd al-Radi's visitors I came across a new face. This was a lad of fifteen to seventeen years. His features were unusually soft and girlish. It made me think of Indian faces. He wore a coat of European origin—perhaps it once belonged to an English soldier—and on his head a gray-brown velvet skullcap (taqiya). Then we sat together with the possessed 'Abd al-Radi. Next to the boy with the Indian face sat the prayer leader of the Naj' al-Hijayri people, who was also the shaykh of the Dandarawi brothers, Muhammad Sulayman. Bakhit predicted to this Muhammad Sulayman that he would yet make the pilgrimage to Mecca, and moreover that this pilgrimage would be especially quick and happy, as if an airplane would transport him to the Holy Places. Muhammad Sulayman was overjoyed at this prospect. Then Muhammad indicated the lad next to him and asked, "Will the Yemeni, our brother akhina, also make another pilgrimage?" Bakhit said, "No, it is not possible." With his hand he pointed to the lad, "This one here, this Yemeni, had a dream. He dreamt that he was sitting with his sister next to water." The lad was quite taken aback by Bakhit's insight into his dream life and took childish pleasure in it. He had really had this dream. Bakhit continued, "This boy is a good fellow, everyone should give him something. He will never return to his home, but will die on the way." The Yemeni nodded agreement with a faint, sad smile.

As we left 'Abd al-Radi, I asked the lad where he would spend the night. Muhammad Sulayman answered for him that he would sleep in the Naj' al-Hijayri mosque where he had slept the night before. I invited him to visit me in Kiman before he continued his journey. He came the next morning. Once again I was enchanted by this soft, gentle, and somewhat tragic child's face. I asked him some questions. He was from the Aden area. His father is a farmer. Father, mother, a brother, and a sister live at home. He left home four years ago. He must have been a child of about twelve years old at the time. Perhaps the family relationships at home were not good. I did not pursue this line of questioning. Muhammad Sulayman had already told me that the boy would quickly begin to cry if one asked him about his parents and siblings. Perhaps homesickness was consuming him. So he left—'ala kayfu—going where he wanted to go, without reason or destination. Old Sanusi, who was sitting with me in the room, fully approved this unpeasantlike wandering 'ala kayfu; it struck him as a God-sent inspiration. He always traveled by foot, never took the train; once or twice he was offered a ride in a car. Going across the desert he carried two gulal clay pots filled with water, hanging from his shoulders. I have met such wanderers in the desert between Qift and Qusayr, whose only baggage was the water jugs over their shoulders. From his home he wandered to the city of Sana'a in South Arabia, thence to Jidda, the port city of the Holy Places. From there he was given a ride by a European in a car until they were close to the border of the Holy Places. He could see a light in the distance, which seemed close but turned out to be very far. This was the light of the Prophet, and shone forth from Mecca. He traveled all night with the European, then got out and wandered further. In Mecca he accomplished the pilgrimage rites. Then he went to Syria. There he fell sick from the strains of wandering. He rested for four months. Then he continued to Iraq, to Baghdad. Because he lacked a passport he was imprisoned and had to wear prison clothing. He stayed in jail for twenty days. He had border problems everywhere, in Syria with the French officials. He gave them information about himself, and said, "I do not lie." And yet he made it through everywhere, often with the help of ordinary soldiers. From Iraq he was deported back to Syria. He continued on from there to Palestine and visited al-Quds, Jerusalem. He saw the churches and the images of the bearded *siyidna 'Isa*—our lord Jesus—and his mother Mariam. He saw how the Christian people prayed in their churches. He stayed four days in Jerusalem. He wanted to stay there and get a job, but he couldn't find one. Then he came to Egypt. In Cairo he met bad days. No one wanted to give him a piece of bread, they all wanted money, and of course he had no money. He couldn't even find a place to sleep. He went to the cemetery. There he slept. In the night he saw ten men; they were the ghosts of pious people. He was afraid. The men said to him, "*Ma takhafsh, ba'da shwaya inta ma'ana*" ("Don't be afraid, soon you will be with us"). That means, "Soon you too will be dead." From Cairo he continued southward, until he reached Naj' al-Hijayri.

When he wants to see his relatives in a dream, before going to sleep he performs ablutions and prayer with this wish in mind, then he sees his people in a dream and speaks with them. The dream that Bakhit had unexpectedly attributed to him the previous day came about in this way. He had dreamed that he and his sister had washed themselves in a brook at home, and had drunk water from it.

I had a favorable impression of this boy. There are plenty of beggars in Egypt avoiding work. He was certainly not one of them. His facial expression was one of pure piety. It seems that this wandering from place to place was just an impatient way to pass the time, an awaiting of the promised death, which would mean a crossing over into another spiritual life plane. And on observing this youth I felt the deep difference between West and East, as if the goal and meaning of a person's life here and there were quite distinct, as if in the East the dividing wall between this world and the other world was very thin, as if the breakthrough point between this world and the far side lies between Egypt and India—in the region of the oldest agrarian high culture. Is it an accident that the great founders of religion all emerged from this region? Through bold meditation one put all earthly and narrow things behind him and found Nirvana; the other, the Son of God, brought the kingdom of the Father to humanity; while the third showed the way out of this world into another, to the merciful Lord of the Worlds.

The Shrine

Two sacred places were created through the incursion of Bakhit—'Abd al-Radi's *khilwa*, his mat-covered place where he sits when the ghosts enter into him, and the *qubba*, the shrine covered with a dome in memory of Bakhit. The *khilwa* is respected for its sacredness, as is shown by the fact that both visitors and 'Abd al-Radi himself remove their shoes before they enter. This is also where 'Abd al-Radi says his prayers when he does not pray in the mosque.

The shrine is a clearer example of sacredness. When Bakhit died many years ago, people set up a ring wall, a *duwar*, in his memory in the courtyard of the house where the family then lived. This house was a few doors away from the present dwelling of 'Abd al-Radi and his father. The wall fell apart and Bakhit was nearly forgotten when he seized 'Abd al-Radi and transformed him into his mount.

We have amply seen the concern of the Upper Egyptian ghosts for a burial memorial. So we can understand that Bakhit in his first public appearance ordered the construction of a *qubba*, a shrine. But Bakhit required even more, that a water fountain and a drinking trough should be set up on the path in front of the house, and a sycamore should be planted. Well and trough should refresh man and beast and the sycamore should provide them shade. Many pious people establish a drinking place on a path—such fountains belong to the image of Upper Egyptian villages and fields. Whether a ghost had already ordered one in this village I do not know, it is certainly possible. But in the case of Bakhit who descended on 'Abd al-Radi and determined to offer his oracles, this order for a fountain and a sycamore is more than a pious gesture: it is a turn toward publicity, an invitation.

Soon after Bakhit's appearance the shrine was built, the sycamore seedling planted, and protected from the scorching sun by durra straw and a wall. The shrine is a whitewashed building with a steep cupola, and covered with paintings. As usual the steep cupola has a couple of tiny windows (see Plate 8). The space inside is always dim. The floor is covered with mats. A niche is halfway up the wall on one side, and contains a lamp; on Muslim holidays and during the festive month of Ramadan, the shrine is lit up every evening. Across the shrine two cords (*mi'lag*, pl. *ma'alig*) are stretched like clotheslines, and on these are hung votive offerings that are brought by those honoring Bakhit. The main content of all such saints' shrines is a wooden 'honor chest' (*tabut*, pl. *tawabit*). The shrine of Bakhit did not yet have this when I came, but during my stay it was acquired and covered over with a beautiful cloth. The interior walls of the sacred spot are also decorated with many pictures and inscriptions.

I now describe the somewhat chaotic decoration of the shrine. The pictures were painted by a lad of about fifteen years, who received not a little praise for his work. The inscriptions were painted by a man who had first vociferously doubted 'Abd al-Radi and his ghost, but was then convinced by the legitimating examples of clairvoyance and became an eager and thankful admirer.

The outside of the shrine is painted and inscribed only on the northern side facing the door and the street. The colors are as unsuitable for the things presented as these things are for a shrine. In order to convey the impression, I describe the colors, pointing out the most common colors in relation to the pictures where they occur (see Plate 9).

Above and to the left, hardly recognizable any more, because the paintings are partly flaked off, we notice a soldier and a camel with the *mahmal* (green and brown). The *mahmal* is a wooden framework covered with an expensive cloth which from time immemorial has been sent by the rulers of Egypt as a gift of honor with the pilgrimage caravan to Mecca. Beneath it, and easier to make out, there is a rider with a lance on a long-legged nag (brown and green), somewhat to the right above it a handprint (blue), under it a teapot (green), to the right of that a goose (green and brown), further to the right a kind of flag (green and brown). There is also a fan made of palm ribs, wrapped in threads. These fans are mostly made in southern Upper Egypt by Nubians, using pretty patterns. People bring them back from their trips to the south; they are showpieces in the color-poor fellah household.

Beneath this row of pictures steams a railroad train (green, blue, and brown), under it a goose (green and yellow), next to it and below— but barely recognizable as such—a ship with a sail high on the peak of the mast (green and brown).

Further down is a broad braid pattern (yellow, green, and brown). This stretches across the whole lower half of the wall with the door.

Just above the door is an inscription: "In the name of God, the merciful, the compassionate. This is the shaykhly memorial of Bakhit Farag Yusuf from Naj' al-Hijayri. The writer is the unworthy 'Awad

'Ali Muhammad 'Awad [from] al-Hijayri." This writer would transform himself; from a Saul he would become a Paul.

On the wooden door is another inscription (green): "This is the place *(maqam)* of Shaykh Bakhit."

Underneath is a goose (brown and green), then a six-pointed Star of David, *gamara*, or moon (brown and green).

To the right of the door, at the very top, at the point of the wall is an inscription (brown): "Written on 15 June 1933."

According to 'Abd al-Radi this is the date on which the inscription was painted. And that was probably right after the completion of the shrine. And the shrine may have been built a month after the first appearance of Bakhit. So we arrive at mid-May (1933) as the probable date for the inception of 'Abd al-Radi's clairvoyance. The writer has unexpectedly given the date according to the Christian, European calendar. He must have thought that would appear refined.

To the right below this there is a bicyclist (brown and green). Bicyclists are a rare and impressive appearance. Then again the Star of David, *gamara* (brown, yellow, and green), above that a man (green). Beneath the *gamara* is a goose (brown and green), to its right a man leading a camel bearing a *mahmal* (green, blue, and brown).

In the row below there is another fan (green, brown, and blue), to the right a handprint (blue), then a saluting soldier (brown and blue)—"he is greeting the train," which is coming from the right.

Then below from the left, a man with a camel and *mahmal* (green, brown, and blue), a rider with a sword (brown and green), and a car (green, brown, and blue).

Under this to the left, but rather smudged, a bicyclist (green and brown) and a goose (brown and green).

The paintings inside the shrine are just as baroque and without any feeling for the effect of colors. There are riders with lances, handprints, soldiers saluting, fans, men with banners—disappearing in the motley array without any relationship to 'Abd al-Radi's call-dream—camel riders, camels with *mahmal*, Stars of David, ships, scorpions, palm trees, cars, bicyclists, rifles, geese, teapots, jugs, a chicken, railroad trains. Scattered in this collection of images are a few pious expressions.

Such strange decorations are found in many memorial shrines of Upper Egyptians saints. This is the style in which the houses of pilgrims are also decorated. From there this decoration is carried over to the shrines. The images relate to the pilgrimage. Thus the camels, sometimes with a *mahmal*, the railroad trains, the ships, the cars, the soldier, the desert riders with their lances. Associated with this are some common linked notions. Striking and perhaps reflecting distinctive origins is the very common bird, drawn here as a goose.

Let us now turn to see what kinds of gifts, especially votive gifts (*nadr*, pl. *nudur*), are hung inside. (see Plate 10) From left to right we see as follows:

1. Fruits of the doum palm. The owner of the palm tree has sent them to Shaykh Bakhit. He had not promised anything to the shaykh; he brought them out of delight over the good harvest and in general to ensure the blessing of Bakhit.

2. A string of dates. This is a present from a woman who remained for a long time without a child. Bakhit had identified a remedy for her. The woman then vowed dates, candles, and gold to Bakhit when she would bear a child, which she did.

3. *Ganadil*, candles, heads of sorghum, brought by a man who had promised this sacrifice if he had a good harvest.

4. A bird made of paper. These birds are sold on feast days as a toy for children. A girl had promised this gift if she got married.

5. A string of dates, from a woman who had received advice from the shaykh to overcome childlessness, and had borne a child. (See no. 2.)

6. The horns of a small male goat. A man and a woman had vowed to sacrifice a goat in honor of Shaykh Bakhit and to celebrate a feast with drums and flute, if they were given a child. A son was born, the feast celebrated, and the horns hung here.

7. Colored cloth threads. Brought by a bride after her marriage. (See no. 4.)

8. A red banner, hemmed in white and on which were sewn two white half moons (crescents). Vowed by an ill man in case of his recovery, and then given.

9. Colored cloths. They were given by a woman after marriage, together with candles and gold. (See nos. 4 and 7.)

10. A little white wooden horse with only one leg, a toy of European origin. This is the present of a man who saw such things in the market of Qena at the festival of the great saint 'Abd al-Rahim. He wanted to

please Shaykh Bakhit with this. This is not a votive gift, but probably a love gift (*mahabba*, pl. *mahabbat*).

11. Dates. (See nos. 2 and 5.)

12. The same.

13. A single head of sorghum. (See no. 3.)

14. A little water bottle, *gulla*. A potter had vowed this to Bakhit if his work turned out to be successful.

When I looked again at these hanging gifts later, there were a couple of new ones, such as a colorful European flower vase and a lamp bulb. These curious gifts were brought by a man who traveled to Cairo after a favorable oracle from Bakhit, and carried out his business successfully. Thankful, he honored the shaykh with this greeting from the big city.

The Priesthood

We have seen how 'Abd al-Radi's possession led to the introduction of a change in peasant society, how there came about a new center represented by 'Abd al-Radi. We have seen how from this center came, with the construction of the shrine and the provision of the trough and the sycamore, a movement toward a public role. And now finally we see how a priesthood emerged here.

'Abd al-Radi himself can be described as a priest, as the priest of the ghost of the deceased Bakhit. He is the chosen one, the intermediary between the living and the dead.

'Abd al-Radi's priesthood is quite individual. Around him we find the beginnings of a family priesthood. 'Abd al-Radi's father, Hamed, the brother of Bakhit, from the outset attempted to appropriate the presents that 'Abd al-Radi received during his possession, arguing that he was Bakhit's brother. 'Abd al-Radi strongly opposed this claim. He was the chosen one and the beloved, the riding camel of the ghost-spirit, and to him were thus due the gifts that Bakhit insisted on for his "camel." Right from the beginning Hamed was brought into the financing of the shrine construction. We have seen that Bakhit in his first appearance demanded that Hamed should pay the cost of the shroud, so that construction could begin with this money. Hamed was associated with the shrine, and so it was only natural that later he became the guard of the holy place and a priest in the shrine. He is the *naqib*, the watchman and the director. Above we have taken note of Hamed's role in the crowd in the waiting area. To this potentially influential post he then added something new. He takes care of the cleaning and lighting of the shrine. He receives his share from the visitors, especially those who bring votive offerings.

Hamed has an even more important priestly function that quite naturally fell to him: He interprets the obscure oracles of the ghost. This is no occasional function of which Hamed is unaware. He is almost always present when people come to consult his son. He gets to know the people in the courtyard where they are waiting, and in many cases he knows why they came. 'Abd al-Radi sees in his possession clairvoyantly the cases of illness, theft, need, for which the client brought him a *riha*. The images from these insights are often dim, the information from them therefore unclear and tentative. Hamed then tries to interpret these fragments from the messages—he is the intermediary between the possessed and the one consulting the oracle. If he knows the case for which the client came, then he can give a meaning to the oracles with some assurance, to respond to the expectations of the asker. On the other hand he works through a correction of the meaning conveyed by the client, to help the possessed find the thread, to help him to grasp the dim images more confidently.

I assume that in the circle of women, 'Abd al-Radi's spouse Fatma plays the role that Hamed plays among the men.

So we see how a family priesthood grows out of the individual one. When 'Abd al-Radi dies, the shrine will remain, and so will the habit of the people to bring their sacrificial gifts, to seek the blessing of the holy man. And with the shrine the priesthood of the family survives.

The usual process would be that after a few generations, Bakhit's shrine would fall apart and the priesthood would be extinguished, because other ghosts would occupy the hearts of men and their shrines would then receive the votive gifts.

But again, such a holy place like that of Bakhit and the priesthood is a nucleus that just might grow out into a great religious center—if a special grace becomes present in the place, and its fame should spread from mouth to mouth, and if clever natural leaders appear in the priestly family.

'Abd al-Radi's Character

L et us now bring up to date the physical impression that 'Abd al-Radi made on us. We can elaborate the picture in a few brushstrokes.

'Abd al-Radi appears weak and suffering. His posture is poor, his back is curved, his shoulders pulled forward. After I got to know him and heard of the long and difficult illness, I thought at first of a case of tuberculosis. His facial color is pale. But that can be explained because, in contrast to other fellahin, 'Abd al-Radi spends most of his time at home in the shade. At the time of research, 'Abd al-Radi was in his early thirties. For his age, he had a good many white hairs in his temples. In his left eye 'Abd al-Radi had a white spot about half the size of a pea on the iris next to the pupil. This spot is said to have been there a while, certainly long before the possession; it probably impairs his vision. During the illness that preceded the possession experience, his right leg and arm became exceptionally thin. Since Bakhit's call these limbs have gradually recovered their normal size. The observer can no longer distinguish the right arm from the left; however, the muscles are weaker, and the grip of the right hand is weaker than that of the left. The right leg, especially in the calf and reaching to the upper thigh at the time of research, was still visibly thinner than the left. In the next section we will hear more about pain in the legs.

We can now turn to examine 'Abd al-Radi's sex life. 'Abd al-Radi married when he was about twenty years old. He lived harmoniously with his wife Fatma. He took pleasure in their sex life. I have probed carefully to see whether this marriage was disturbed in any way through inhibitions or disputes. It was not. 'Abd al-Radi was married only to Fatma. Neither before nor after the marriage had he known another woman. Nevertheless, 'Abd al-Radi's sex life had to bear the burden of the long annual absences that kept him from his wife for months, when he was a worker in Isma'iliya before the onset of the illness. The longest period he spent away from his wife was precisely before the onset of the greatest illness. I asked 'Abd al-Radi about his sex life in Isma'iliya, in such a way that it would have been easy for him to admit visiting prostitutes. Spontaneously, smiling, and with firmness he said had not visited whores. With the sexual drive he had felt normally—'Abd al-Radi underlined his words with a gesture of his bent arm—he had had nocturnal emissions. If he saw a tempting woman, this second Joseph would shield his eyes with his headscarf. Now that 'Abd al-Radi had recuperated from the big illness he was certainly a new person, chosen by the ghosts to be a medium. And a deep change entered into the essential expression of his sex life: Although his body was regaining strength, the sexual urge, and also any need for sexual relationships, was denied to him. Once I asked 'Abd al-Radi if earlier, before the shaykh descended on him, he had been happier, if he wished for this new circumstance to end so that he could again be like other men, if above all he wished once again to enjoy sexual pleasures. 'Abd al-Radi gave a firm negative answer to all these questions. He feels himself happy in his new circumstances. Finally he said to me, since we were touching on sex life, that the body is transitory and would turn to dust, while among the ghosts, with whom he was now dealing, there was nothing transitory. His shaykh Bakhit is a blessing (baraka), a grace from God. His wife, said 'Abd al-Radi, was certainly sad because of this loss, but thank God, they already had two children. Insofar as an outside observer like me could form an opinion, I had the impression that until today the relationship between 'Abd al-Radi and his Fatma remains harmonious. He loves her and she loves him. We must remember that it was above all Fatma who cared for him when he was completely helpless. This would have strengthened an already good marriage. And today Fatma holds the same shy and joyous reverence for Shaykh Bakhit as 'Abd al-Radi himself.

People were once talking about ghosts in the presence of 'Abd al-Radi; a rather obscene story of a ghost was told (see p. 30). 'Abd al-Radi was in no way shocked but smiled in amusement. When on another occasion I was showing him pictures of pretty Algerian girls from a catalog, he looked at them indifferently, while a couple of photos of a scenic group of palm trees, and of bearded Muslim scholars that were next to the pictures of the seductive women, attracted his attention and delight.

To this overall picture corresponds 'Abd al-Radi's childishness. Once when I was feeling his pulse, and then had him feel his own pulse, I explained to him how the heart is the pump for blood circulation, and said that when the heart stops beating the man is dead. This explanation that a man goes when the heart stops gave him innocent pleasure.

Once when 'Abd al-Radi was visiting me in Kiman, he saw on my table a toy from a peasant child. This was a roughly constructed camel made from fired clay. I had had stirrups made and a guide rope from bits of string as an experiment for myself. 'Abd al-Radi picked up this figure in his hand twice, and clearly took pleasure in it. The stirrups and guide rope added to his enjoyment. He argued that I should now put a rider on the animal. With the same childlike interest he noted the mixture of wall decorations that my assistant had introduced into the room. The good Mahdi had stuck up on the wall pages from illustrated magazines with store models on one half, a bearded Swiss cotton merchant and an Egyptian lady on the other half. There were also postcards, a picture of King Fuad, a sleeping infant recommending Nestle's milk powder, and more. He looked at one picture after another, astonished and delighted.

The enjoyment of pictures is characteristic of 'Abd al-Radi and may be of importance to understanding his clairvoyance. Once I was sitting next to 'Abd al-Radi in his room. Conversation was going this way and that. We were speaking of songs. I asked him what he preferred, songs or pictures. Unhesitatingly and rather childishly came the answer: pictures. One day I presented him with the catalog in which the pictures of the pretty Algerian girls, the landscape, and the scholars' heads could be seen, and he took exceptional pleasure in this. He was even happier when I brought him two color prints from Cairo, the kind you can buy from street peddlers. One showed Adam and Eve, the other showed

Imam 'Ali striking down a demon, *jinni*. The grotesque demon wore a colorful neckband with glimmers of gold, and was carrying a decorative club, a thin yellow staff with a club head that was not completely round, adorned with a couple of multicolored stripes. 'Abd al-Radi was much more interested in the demon than in the hero 'Ali. 'Abd al-Radi proclaimed immediately that the demon was a *zar* spirit "because he has a necklace." When this idea, that it was an image of a *zar* spirit, began to grow, he now identified the club head as a hand drum and the yellow club staff as a flute. In *zar* ceremonies there is ecstatic music. The identification was not suggested in any way by the drawing, bad as it was. A fellah tried to give a better reading, pointing out that the sphere could not be a drum and the yellow staff a flute, that both together formed a club. In vain: 'Abd al-Radi's horizons were narrow, he saw only individual parts, small sections, not the whole. And the amazing thing was that he was able to persuade his critic of his mistaken viewpoint. This limited horizon, this isolation of partial impressions, may be important for 'Abd al-Radi's vision. I had to reflect how, when he was in a state of possession, he would take the *riha* in hand and then select excerpts from a picture of illness or a story of theft and then would feel for other images, to seek to broaden out what had already been found. We can recall here the remarkable mystical verses from the saints circling in the desert, which 'Abd al-Radi occasionally and solemnly recited while in possession: these too are of course parts of a whole, images of the moment.

We can also reflect on the piety of 'Abd al-Radi. 'Abd al-Radi had always been a good Muslim, if not perhaps unusually devout. He never took part in *zikr* ceremonies. He was only an onlooker. It is significant that he let the image of the *zikr* work on him. Earlier he did not believe that ghosts *(mashayikh)* could manifest themselves in humans, he had never visited a possessed person, and when he was advised during this illness to seek out such a person and present his *riha*, he refused. It would have been important to know more about the religiosity of his wife Fatma and her beliefs in ghostly spirits. There could have been influences from this side.

Since 'Abd al-Radi was taken over by a ghost, he feels himself as a chosen one, as extraordinary. This we have already seen. And therefore his piety is now even greater. He prays regularly, and according to pious usage he has left an unshaven topknot on his shaven skull. This top knot is called *guttiya*. People let it grow so that when the corpse is washed the head can be held: in other words, it is a permanent memento mori. He keeps fasts carefully, even the individual fasts that Bakhit commands. 'Abd al-Radi does not smoke. Earlier he had occasionally smoked a cigarette or two, but has stopped now that he supports a ghost. In this way he follows the practice of the Dandarawiya brothers, who frown on the use of tobacco. The Dandarawiya have many adherents in Naj' al-Hijayri. 'Abd al-Radi often mentions one of the names of God—*ya rabb* (O Lord God), *ya mawjud* (O the existing), *ya karim* (O the generous). 'Abd al-Radi mentions these names especially in breaks in the conversation, often with a sigh. I had the impression that his thoughts were roaming far away and that they returned to us when the name of God is invoked. When the name of Muhammad is mentioned in conversation, 'Abd al-Radi never omits to murmur the conventional blessing for the messenger of God.

To conclude, here is my personal overall impression. 'Abd al-Radi is a pure soul. Lying and cheating are far from him. His being is shy and gentle. He lives with the peace of soul of a devout person. He is not after gain, although he did tell his ghost that he would have to live thanks to his blessing. He is thankful for the honoraria he receives while in possession, and for which he sometimes asks.

'Abd al-Radi's Subjective Relationship to his Ghostly Spirits

'A bd al-Radi experiences the onset of possession as falling asleep. When he awakes, he feels his heart beating strongly and a pounding in the temples. Everything around him—the walls, the people—spins. He feels as if he has been shattered. In particular he can sense the aftereffects of the pressure of the ghosts on his shoulders and the front thorax—'Abd al-Radi laid both hands under the nipples in order to show me—and in the knees. 'Abd al-Radi's legs hurt, especially after a lengthy possession. As he says, this is because Bakhit obliges him to remain on his knees as a young camel. Both legs are painful, not just the right one. After a very lengthy session, 'Abd al-Radi staggered out of his *khilwa* with small, slow, weary steps and a very bent-over upper body and a deathly tired face.

Bakhit presses as hard as a stone, but Shaykh 'Ali of Naj' al-Hijayri presses even harder. He is the one who announces himself through tightly folded arms. He often pushes 'Abd al-Radi back into the wall. When he awakes, 'Abd al-Radi feels as if there were knife pricks in his back. On the other hand, Muhammad 'Abd al-Qadir of Barahma, the ghost of the man who was run over by a train, is agreeably light. 'Abd al-Radi's mother's brother, 'Abdallah, is also quite gentle.

In spite of the imprint that the ghosts sitting on his shoulders leave—he is, after all, the young camel—'Abd al-Radi maintains that

145

ghosts enter into him themselves and are in his body during the possession. I asked 'Abd al-Radi if Bakhit enters into him through his mouth or his nose. I told him that once toward the end of a possession, he had picked at his nose and then said, "Get out." 'Abd al-Radi knew nothing of this, nor did he know how the ghosts entered into him.

We have seen that the great experience of 'Abd al-Radi that changed everything was the call-dream in which Bakhit appeared and held out to him a flag. We also saw how all the possible images that came later, perhaps also in the form of dreams, were built on this call-dream. 'Abd al-Radi was very guarded in the portrayal of his inner life, his dreams, his thoughts about the ghostly spirits. Only after long acquaintance, only after he was sure that I took him seriously and was linked to him as a friend, did he occasionally speak of this. It was as if he momentarily pulled aside a curtain with which he also hid these images from himself and his waking consciousness.

'Abd al-Radi sees Bakhit every Tuesday eve (the evening before Tuesday). And in fact he always sees him in the company of many people. He is performing *zikr* with them—*A(llah) A(llah) A(llah)*. Since the call-dream, Bakhit has never spoken to 'Abd al-Radi. In such dreams, 'Abd al-Radi took part in the *zikr* with Bakhit and his crew. Once Bakhit in a dream (not the call-dream) gave him a green cloth. When I probed more about this dream, 'Abd al-Radi became shy and silent. He whispered, "These dreams are only between Bakhit and me. Shaykh Bakhit does not like me to speak of them to anyone." This discretion confirms for me the purity of Bakhit.

The ghosts love the desert, and they often hold their *zikr*s there. As 'Abd al-Radi was telling me of this, he was returning from a condolence call in the town of Qus. Unexpectedly and without prompting he then said, "The ghosts are also sometimes in Qus."

One Friday eve, 'Abd al-Radi saw the Aswan cemetery in a dream, surrounded by a high wall. There were innumerable shaykhs' shrines, and at the end he also saw the shrine of Shaykh 'Ada. All the shrines were lit up in a wonderful soft green light. A broad beautiful street led up from the Nile to this cemetery. 'Abd al-Radi has never been in Aswan. Aswan for him is a mystical concept, a place for ghosts. In Aswan there are indeed a considerable number of saints' shrines. 'Abd al-Radi had probably heard this somewhere, and the image of an Aswan full of shrines has been taken over by him as the image of the place of ghosts. Shaykh 'Ada, who today is being adopted by the 'Azayza in Kiman, certainly has no shrine in distant Aswan. But here in the Qift cemetery his sanctuary-grave stands in a corner at the far side of the graves, and this situation is carried over into 'Abd al-Radi's dream imagery. The shrine of Shaykh 'Ada stands as the last one. Once when I asked 'Abd al-Radi where his Bakhit would be, if not in him, the answer came promptly, "In Aswan, all the saints (*wali*, pl. *awliya*) are in Aswan!" Another time 'Abd al-Radi said that Shaykh Bakhit is in "paradise with God." He would beat him, 'Abd al-Radi, if he drank wine. When I told him that Bakhit must be in Aswan, he quickly agreed with me, but then immediately added that he is "in paradise with God." This Aswan is not the Upper Egyptian city of Aswan, but a heavenly Aswan, perhaps a location in paradise itself.

Bakhit is together on the far side with twenty-four saints (*awliya*); he is their leader. All of them can descend on him, 'Abd al-Radi, Bakhit's young camel mount. Twenty-four is a nominal figure and denotes 'many.' No one has counted how many ghosts have descended on 'Abd al-Radi; no one will count them. When I asked 'Abd al-Radi how he knew there were twenty-four, he attributed this information to the call-dream, saying this is when Bakhit told him this.

The Relationship Between 'Abd al-Radi's Waking Consciousness and the Possession Situation

For 'Abd al-Radi it is an unshakable truth that Bakhit himself and other ghostly spirits enter into him. Many of his visitors also hold fast to this belief. Others may doubt, but the doubt does not concern the factuality of the spirits, but only the type of spirits. They think that demons, not ghosts, are present in 'Abd al-Radi when he is possessed.

We modern Europeans doubt that spirits manifest themselves, doubt above all that there are spirits in the first place. We only relax when we bring such spirit appearances into accord with our worldview, based on a close observation of nature. It is our right and duty to maintain such reflection, for this is our special accomplishment, and only because of it did Europe become great.

It is of decisive importance to determine whether there are links between 'Abd al-Radi's waking consciousness and the possession situation, between 'Abd al-Radi's waking personality and the personalities taken up during possession.

First of all, we set out the distinction between these circumstances.

'Abd al-Radi remembers nothing, after a possession episode, of what his mouth articulated, nothing of what he did or heard.

When Bakhit was handling 'Abbas, who was suspected of being possessed (p. 123), he applied a paste to the skull of the sick youth. When 'Abd al-Radi woke up from possession, he saw a few drops of this paste on the ground. With surprise, he asked what that was, and he required a detailed explanation.

Among the ghosts there once appeared Salim of Hu (pp. 100–101), known for chasing away cats. A couple of days later, 'Abd al-Radi was in my house in Kiman, and I asked him about this shaykh. He first had to remember that there was such a shaykh, and he remembered nothing about cats and frightening them away. He was amazed to learn that this shaykh had entered into him.

I had photographed 'Abd al-Radi in a state of possession (see p. ii and Plates 2–7). He knew certainly later about other photos that I had taken of him in a waking state, but he couldn't remember at all that his picture in a state of possession had been taken. Nevertheless, it entered into his consciousness during possession that he would be photographed, as we will show later.

Let us now observe the bridges between 'Abd al-Radi's waking consciousness and the possession state.

Before the sessions, especially the afternoon ones, 'Abd al-Radi would often sit in the forecourt among the guests. Thus it might happen that here and there he might ask for news of another. Occasionally he asked my assistant whether I had received any letters, what kind of news there was, or what my plans for the immediate future were. These cautious questions appear very suspicious, but our mistrust disappears at once, for 'Abd al-Radi is not asking secretly, but without consideration for the presence of others whom it might concern; in fact he frequently asked them directly. It is not the case that he seeks out news behind the back of a client in order to bring it forth later during possession as an example of clairvoyance. 'Abd al-Radi instinctively incorporates such information, which sinks into another level of consciousness and can be an indicator on the path when he seeks for visions of the distant.

Once when 'Abd al-Radi was visiting me in Kiman and we were having a friendly conversation, he said to me, "When you go to Cairo, please bring me blue and white striped cloth for a robe." A few days later, I visited him. He passed into possession, Bakhit appeared and addressed me. At the end he said, "The gentleman will bring a robe from Cairo for the young camel."

Another time I had brought 'Abd al-Radi a packet of candles. On this day the shaykh did not come down at all. The candles were intended to light Bakhit's shrine. A couple of days later, Bakhit announced, while in possession of 'Abd al-Radi, "The gentleman there has given me candles."

Furthermore, one can mention that during possession 'Abd al-Radi somehow feels what is happening around him. For instance, he senses where a guest sits who would like to offer him a *riba*. 'Abd al-Radi was also aware while possessed that I was photographing him. First of all, the onset of possession was delayed when I had my camera with me, and when the possession was underway, I could feel clearly in the gestures and speech of 'Abd al-Radi some inhibitions that grew when he turned to me or in the direction where I sat. In fact, 'Abd al-Radi once opened his otherwise half-shut eyes and glanced fleetingly at my place with veiled gaze.

Finally, 'Abd al-Radi told me on one of his visits to Kiman of the gestures of the ghosts. We were in the middle of an intimate conversation, in which he was speaking to me of his dreams, as a friend. He said then, "When Shaykh 'Ali descends, he crosses his arms. Shaykh Khalifa Mustafa and Shaykh 'Abdallah sit with their legs crossed under them." We have seen that some of the ghosts make themselves clear through very particular body language or gestures—Bakhit throughout, for whom 'Abd al-Radi hastened to sit upright on his knees, the singing al-Asyuti through the raised right hand, Muhammad 'Abd al-Qadir because he always stroked himself across his chest, meaning that he had been run over. It is remarkable that 'Abd al-Radi outside possession knew about these gestures. I remember, in fact, that he confided this in me while we were in a confidential conversation, whispering together; it seemed as though both of us had dropped down into another level of 'Abd al-Radi's consciousness.

Links between 'Abd al-Radi's waking consciousness and the state of possession certainly exist. Let us now look at a particular complex of images evoked during possession.

In messages given to me personally Bakhit described my house in Germany and its situation (p. 105). On February 15, Bakhit portrayed the house situation in a garden, with trees across from the garden gate. This corresponds to reality. He then described further how my son was sliding back and forth between the house door and the garden gate. This could have meant a sledding track and thus correspond to reality. He mentioned a water pump in the house that in fact is not there. The entire session dealt with this personal message to me.

In a session on March 2, first Bakhit appeared, then al-Asyuti, who sang, then Muhammad 'Abd al-Qadir from Barahma, who whispered with his father, who was present, and began to sing happily. Then Bakhit appeared. He turned to me, portrayed my family, and evoked through gestures the situation of the house in the garden. This time there was no mention of a pump. Shortly afterward—still concerned with me—Bakhit recited the mystical poem on the wandering saints. Then Bakhit turned his attention to another.

In a third session, on March 25, which was once again occupied with a message directed to me, Bakhit portrayed first of all my family, then with a gesture he indicated the street, then the house and its door. Next to the house the pump appeared again, with flowing water. Then the trees were briefly mentioned. Then he added that there was a railroad near the house, and there were also pigeons flying around the house. Immediately after concluding this portrayal, 'Abd al-Radi again recited the mystical poem. In reality there are no pigeons near my house in Germany.

We can break down this complex of images into two parts. In the desert, half an hour north of Naj' al-Hijayri, a Swiss, Mr. J. Dudler,[9] had built a house. This house is situated inside a large courtyard surrounded by a high wall. Especially on the northern side are planted a few bushes. To supply this house with water, a well was dug and a pump fitted to it. On the wall, on the southern gate side, is a dovecote.

This house has influenced 'Abd al-Radi's vision of my house in Tübingen. The Swiss and I are Europeans. Here in the isolation of Qift and its villages this is a rare occurrence. In the consciousness of every peasant, Mr. Dudler and I are placed in the same category.

In his possession 'Abd al-Radi saw in his vision my house in Tübingen. The portrayal of the house with trees in the garden, and the youngster sledding back and forth on the track, do not correspond to Dudler's house, but to mine.

---

9 Joseph Dudler was a Swiss mining entrepreneur working to locate and exploit mines in Egypt's Eastern Desert. He lived in the house with his wife and ten-year-old son. He and Winkler were friendly. See Winkler, *Ägyptische Volkskunde*, 1936, pp. 51, 66. NSH

In the second session the portrayal of the house was abbreviated, the pump was left out. Immediately after the description of the house, 'Abd al-Radi recited the poem on the saints wandering in the desert. The inclusion of these lines in the third session following again the description of the house I consider part of the complex. They had been available in 'Abd al-Radi's consciousness for a long time. Now they surfaced, because the image of my house recalled the image of Dudler's house, which lies in the desert where the saints roam.

In the third session the house is once again supplied with a pump. But something new has been added in the form of the nearby railroad and the pigeons flying around the house. The mystical poem was again recited. The pigeons derive from the image of Dudler's house, while the railroad comes from the image of my house in Germany.

This sequence of images is remarkable. In his vision, 'Abd al-Radi first established the image of my house. This image was obscured by the image of Dudler's house from 'Abd al-Radi's waking consciousness. It is as if a photographer had developed two images on the same plate, first my house, then Dudler's. The picture that the photographer took of my house is now on the plate, but it is not clear; it is marred by the superimposed images of the other house.

We can refer a complex of forms to this complex of images.

When 'Abd al-Radi was supposed to heal 'Abbas (p. 100), Bakhit was the first to appear, then 'Ali of the crossed arms from Naj' al-Hijayri, who was muttering to himself, "reciting from the Qur'an," then al-Asyuti who sang, then Wardani with the crossed legs from Kiman, who was whispering the *Fatiha* to himself, then 'Abd al-Qadir al-Jilani, who sang cheerfully, then Salim of Hu appeared, and finally Bakhit.

I bring up this sequence of ghostly spirits once again to show that there is a pattern: 'Ali and Wardani, al-Asyuti and Jilani, correspond to each other, and Wardani appears as the double of 'Ali, and Jilani of al-Asyuti. 'Ali and al-Asyuti are ghosts/spirits who frequently appear. Wardani and Jilani very seldom appear, I only knew of them in this case. The pair of 'Ali who whispers and al-Asyuti who sings produced, so to speak, its mirror image, Wardani who whispers and Jilani who sings.

I did not observe any other such parallelism, for it is rare that so many ghosts appear one after the other. The parallel sequences could be an accident, or it could be a reduplication that suggests the creation of a new spirit. As such it shines light into the mechanics of the possession events.

As far as my material extends, one can observe the traces of an order inside the spirit experience. Al-Asyuti likes to appear near Shaykh 'Ali—indeed, we found the two adjacent to each other. And the ghostly spirit of the crushed Muhammad 'Abd al-Qadir of Barahma comes in the sequence of appearances near that of Shaykh 'Ali. In one session appeared Muhammad 'Abd al-Qadir, then Shaykh 'Ali, then al-Asyuti; in another al-Asyuti preceded Muhammad 'Abd al-Qadir; and in a third al-Asyuti was followed by Shaykh 'Ali, then again by al-Asyuti.

The bridging links between 'Abd al-Radi's waking consciousness and the possession situation act to shake our belief in the reality of ghostly spirits in the broader sense. We see that in one level of 'Abd al-Radi's consciousness his normal waking personality and the dream personality meet. We see moreover that in individual cases, "ghosts" who present themselves with names can simply be explained as the reflections of already available older forms. This in turn makes it possible that all the appearances that manifest themselves in 'Abd al-Radi are only aspects of his self, that no foreign ghosts came from outside to enter him. It is important for us now to reach the level of 'Abd al-Radi's consciousness where the possessing spirits exist. I remember that 'Abd al-Radi, in the intimate conversations in my room in Kiman, spoke to me of his dreams in which he saw his shaykh Bakhit and performed *zikr* exercises with him and his crew. 'Abd al-Radi told me—again in such a serious, intimate conversation—that he had dreams by night that took him away, to other villages, to al-Shaykhiya or Barahma. There he could see everything. These are pleasant dreams. He told me twice that he had visited my house in Germany in a dream. And 'Abd al-Radi went on to portray, now in waking consciousness, the house exactly as he described it when possessed by Bakhit. Now in one of the dreams he also saw me in my home with my children. The children were playing. As a good Muslim he did not mention my wife in this context. He could see there a tree, and moreover the water pump. He had barely told me this much, then he said that he could not speak more of this beautiful dream. He covered his mouth with his hand and held it closed.

We heard that 'Abd al-Radi participated in *zikr*s neither before nor after the call; he was only present as a spectator. But in the dream 'Abd al-Radi takes part with Bakhit and his crew, and at the beginning of possession episodes Bakhit himself frequently performs *zikr* in that he breathes out the three short breaths.

'Abd al-Radi once organized a *zikr*. It was on a beautiful moonlit night. The *zikr* participants stood in two rows in front of 'Abd al-Radi's house with the *munshid* between the rows. The *munshid* swayed his body rhythmically to and fro, bent his head far backward and then threw it forward. He sang in a loud, already hoarse voice full of deep conviction. At first the *zikr* brothers recited the word *Allah*, led by the *munshid* with his singing and hand clapping. Then followed the *zikr* theme *Allah hay*, "God is living." Then followed silent breathing exercises, progressively wilder and more exciting. Occasionally the wheezing breath of a brother sounded out, like the sobbing of a woman. This devotion of all the brothers had an absolutely feminine effect, this sobbing seemed like an ecstatic scream. The *munshid* had a masculine effect, dominating the others with song and rhythm. 'Abd al-Radi did not take part in this *zikr*. He watched it. When the brothers began to do their silent *zikr* breathing, he had his incense pot brought and censed the brothers mightily. I see in this some kind of a parallel behavior to the dream behavior, when Bakhit appears in possession. Possession is introduced with incense, then Bakhit appears in 'Abd al-Radi and performs the *zikr* breathing exercises.

In conclusion, we can return to 'Abd al-Radi's call-dream once again. Certainly Bakhit had largely been forgotten when 'Abd al-Radi was afflicted with his serious illness. But 'Abd al-Radi was then a man of more than thirty years. He had often enough during this period heard of Bakhit, most probably in early childhood, the time that lay very near to the death of the historical Bakhit. So 'Abd al-Radi in the course of his life could have slowly accumulated the raw material that now became the possession circumstances for Bakhit—memories of the external appearance, the speaking style, and the life practices of Bakhit, together with anecdotes of his doings. The legitimation of Bakhit through 'Abd al-Radi's story from his own childhood of how he stole pomegranates might impress the fellahin, but it is not enough for us.

It is noteworthy in the call-dream that Bakhit appeared to 'Abd al-Radi and held out a banner to him. Whence this image? On the way from Naj' al-Hijayri to Kiman and Qift there is an isolated double sanctuary. Since childhood 'Abd al-Radi often passed this way, whether heading for the fields or the market. The sanctuary in fact plays no special role, at least in 'Abd al-Radi's family. But whoever passes by this solitary shrine quite naturally glances at the door opening onto the road. And above this door one can see a rough drawing, brown in color. It shows a man who is holding a banner. Next to it is also a blurred drawing of something like a tree (see Plate 11). The picture of this man with the banner above the sanctuary door, together with one to whom he is handing the banner, who is entering into sacred space, catches the attention of the passerby, and catches his attention even more when the gaze passes fleetingly over the door. I think that this is the original image that determined 'Abd al-Radi's call-dream. Later, when I showed 'Abd al-Radi a photograph of this shrine door with the painting, he did not recall that he had ever seen it. This confirms my assumption that this image has penetrated down into the dream level of his consciousness.

Conclusion

We have attempted to demystify 'Abd al-Radi's ghosts. We have partially succeeded. Our acceptance has been shattered in a couple of places, when we were able to explain Bakhit on the basis of 'Abd al-Radi's old memories, the call-dream as the expression of an image in a shrine wall painting, a couple of ghosts as mirror images of others. In no case was it compellingly proven that there were ghosts who entered into 'Abd al-Radi from the outside. So we can doubt that any spirits whatsoever penetrated 'Abd al-Radi, and we are also skeptical that ghosts exist in the first place.

But not so fast. If we lack proof that spirits exist, we also lack proof to show the Egyptian peasants that ghosts do not exist. We have nothing to show that in reality the ghost of the simple-minded Bakhit did not develop a love for 'Abd al-Radi, choose him as a mount, and descend upon him. We have nothing to show that the ghost of the accidentally killed Muhammad 'Abd al-Qadir did not enter into 'Abd al-Radi in order to console his parents. I think we must seek such a proof with equal rigor.

If Bakhit and the other spirits in 'Abd al-Radi are really only aspects of 'Abd al-Radi's personality, then one dimension is truly wonderful. These split personalities have a completely different and infinitely more extensive field of vision than 'Abd al-Radi in his waking consciousness.

157

This split Bakhit looks through visitors like glass and sees their thoughts. This Bakhit can take a thread from the robe of a sick person, who might be a couple of hundred kilometers away in his sickbed, and this thread in the hand brings into the internal vision of Bakhit the image of the patient, and even more—insight into the cause and treatment of the illness. This Bakhit looks across seas and mountains to Tübingen, thousands of kilometers away from Upper Egypt, and finds at this distance among all the towns and villages a particular town, and among all the houses of this town a particular house, and sees in this house a small girl playing with her doll carriage, precisely the same girl of whom his visitor wished to hear. He sees her with the doll carriage, something that neither the historical Bakhit nor 'Abd al-Radi had ever laid eyes on, something that the questioning interlocutor did not at all suspect might be with the little girl— but that this girl at this hour really had in her hand.

What gives us the right not to trust such a seer—of visions of what in our eyes are quite strange worlds, the world of ghostly spirits? And is there such a large step to concluding that ghostly spirits from this other world penetrate into the seer?

When Muhammad 'Abd al-Qadir appeared in 'Abd al-Radi, he told his elderly father what was being served for dinner the last time he left home. Perhaps the clairvoyant—if we don't want to challenge clairvoyance—could read that in the thoughts of the old man. But he asked him further whether he lost his life because of "God's orders," an accident, or a criminal act. And the ghost gave the answer straightaway. The ghost then continued, saying that the parents should not cry over him any more, as their tears made his cheeks sore. So the ghost suffers and cannot free himself as long as the thoughts of his relatives do not set him free. Does that not fall outside simple clairvoyance?

Such victims of violent death frequently appear in such possessed ones, such as my 'Abd al-Radi. Is this coincidental? Such victims are much closer to people, much more involved in their everyday life, and accustomed to their cares, than those who meet death slowly on a sickbed or through the twilight of old age.

From a totally different perspective, our defense of the reality of spirits approaches popular observation. When a man dies violently the place of his death becomes haunted. The Egyptian peasant is not the only one who has seen such ghosts—this is known around the world at all times.

One more point. When 'Abd al-Radi was about to be possessed, he had to yawn a great deal. He let the incense work on him: This facilitated the onset of possession, which then broke over him like a wave that threatened to drown him. What does that have to do with a split personality? Is this not really a breath, a spirit, in him, which for a couple of moments uses the respiratory tract, so that air cannot simultaneously enter in, and threatens to smother or drown him?

I think it is contrary to the spirit of our science to close our eyes to the possibility of the existence of ghostly spirits.

We want to assume for once their reality. Then we see what an enormous role they play in the religious life of the fellahin. We note that the religiosity of the fellahin of our area is quite different from what we used to think. We thought they were Muslims, believed that what is found in the scholarly books of Muslim theologians corresponds to the thought of these peasants. But no, the ghosts, who according to all the scholars wait in their graves for Judgment Day, are restless; they send illness and death, they demand proper tombs, they are concerned about the well-being of their orphans. So then are the fellahin not good Muslims after all? Are they pagan? Not at all. They are overwhelmingly excellent Muslims. It is precisely here, among these peasants, that we can appreciate the powerful achievement of Muhammad, that we can see why Islam is so alive. Muslim theologians would not be happy with many of these fellahin. But Muhammad would be overjoyed. Muhammad knew God, the merciful Master of the Worlds, origin and goal of all being. And our fellahin also recognize this. 'Abd al-Radi always uttered the profession of faith on awaking from possession: There is no God but God, and Muhammad is his Prophet. And when Bakhit entered into him and took up his place and spoke through his mouth, the first words to come out were remembrances of God and his Prophet. 'Abd al-Radi regularly performed his prayers, he fasted, he murmured the names of God when he sensed that He was before him. He is a good Muslim, a very good Muslim. And that protects him, and protects his fellow countrymen, from any terrible tyranny from these ghosts. God is the depth in the worldview of these fellahin; next to this depth the ghosts are beneficent or unpleasant, in either case rather unimportant beings. Thinking of God, and further the security of belief in God, provides the fellahin with peace in the face of death.

We marvel at these fellahin, who deal so much with ghostly spirits, and even more at 'Abd al-Radi, on whom they descend. The fellah does not find that marvelous. We discover here a deep difference between the structure of our personality and theirs. The fellah—and in this tableau he can stand for a great part of humanity—is in his personality much less solid; the spirits can enter into him, while they cannot enter into us, or at any rate much less often. The walls that support our personality are thicker and higher. The fellah is more modest, satisfied, and content than we in his close relationship to the spirits. We are more alone and restless in the walls of our soul. But in counterpart, we have a protected space where in cool thought and reckoning we can grapple with the cosmos and dominate it. Our way to God is more arduous than theirs, but it leads to an even greater insight.

Index

161

Ghost Riders *of* Upper Egypt

In 1933 the German anthropologist
Hans Alexander Winkler came across
a 'spirit medium' named 'Abd al-Radi
in a village near Luxor in Upper
Egypt. 'Abd al-Radi was periodically
possessed by the ghost of his uncle,
and in that state passed messages to
those who came to seek help. In an
intense study, Winkler lays out the
construction of the world shared by
the rural people, with its saints and
pilgrims, snake charmers and wander-
ing holy men, all under the overarching power of God. Winkler's
book was ahead of its time in analyzing a single institution in its
social context, and in showing the debates and disagreements about
the meaning of such strange events.

"This multilayered study from the 1930s was precocious in its
method and conclusions, and thus it retains its relevance today not
only for Egyptian folklore but also for the history of anthropology
in Egypt."   —from the Introduction by Nicholas S. Hopkins

HANS ALEXANDER WINKLER (1900–45), a German anthropologist
and specialist in comparative religion, received his PhD from the
University of Tübingen.

NICHOLAS S. HOPKINS is emeritus professor of anthropology at
the American University in Cairo.

The American University in Cairo Press

ISBN 978-977-416-250-3

9 789774 162503